ENDORSEMENTS

Dr. Newman's *Call Home* gives us practical ways to engage with this passage and invites us to joyfully bring prayer into the rhythms of everyday life. The book is both encouraging and deeply challenging as we are reminded to stay faithful in intimate communication with God.

Bobby Gruenewald, CEO – YouVersion Bible App,
Innovation Leader & Pastor, Life Church

What a wonderful title for a book! While the words "call home" can bring anxiety, as in "I wonder if something is wrong," but the experience can also bring messages of warmth, love, joy, invitation, information, and even just a "miss you." This book is about prayer, and prayer is simply talking with God and to God, a conversation. In other words, it's about "calling home." I have been familiar with prayer all my life as we were taught to pray for everything, and this is not the case in far too many homes. That's why this book is so needed in today's world. Enjoy your walk through the Lord's Prayer.

Barbara Green
Hobby Lobby Co-Founder

Like a hot cup of coffee, Keith awakened me by reminding us God doesn't send our calls directly to his voicemail. I appreciate Keith's gentle and practical challenge to be more disciplined in my prayer life to gain more freedom with God, my Father.

Nico Gomez, Chief Executive Officer
Bethany Children's Health Center

Prayer is a powerful tool in keeping life sane here on earth for us, fickle humans. God knew that so he taught us to pray by giving us The Lord's Prayer. Keith uses his life experiences and Biblical truths about prayer to make the case to the reader how much God wants us to pray. And like any sports skill, if you learn as much as you can about it and practice praying every day, the results will be transformational. Keith teaches and preaches in the pages of this book like a good coach – encouraging the reader to be their best for a God worthy of our best.

**Shirley Hoogstra, J.D. President,
Council for Christian Colleges and Universities**

Wow, Keith stepped on my toes! In his book *Call Home*, I was both challenged and convicted. You see, I endeavor to be a "real" Christ follower, yet I realize I don't call home as I should. The text is incredible, but the questions may be even better. We all need to read and heed.

**Dr. Lee Roland
Executive Director, Hope United**

As one who has long sought counsel on how to have a more meaningful prayer life, *Call Home* is a most welcome addition to the library of works on the subject. This well-written volume is both personal and practical. The writer brings in experiences from his ministry and family life that illuminate how intimate communication with God can bring divine wisdom and reassurance at times of joy and stress. It is practical and helpful as it is written where we as seekers live day by day. Without reservation I recommend it to anyone who desires a closer relationship with their Creator.

Dr. Loren P. Gresham
President Emeritus, Southern Nazarene University

Call Home provides an insightful invitation to live in a relationship with God – a relationship filled with the desire to listen and speak to God as the Father who is near. Keith's fresh look at the Lord's Prayer moves the reader from the prayer's familiar words to the joy of being in a personal relationship with God himself. *Call Home* will change how you pray and your desire to pray.

Dr. Bob Brower
President, Point Loma Nazarene University

As Jesus commanded us to pray this prayer, Keith brings this classic into our current time and our daily lives. A fresh insight that we all need to read... and to pray.

Rev. Jay Height
Executive Director, Shepherd Community

We are given examples and instructions for prayer in the Bible, but how does that fit in my chaotic world? Challenges at work and home can get in the way of my prayer life. Keith breaks down the Lord's Prayer in *Call Home*, explaining how this time can be spent on a personal, intimate level on a daily, hourly, and continual basis in our stressful, busy life.

Dr. Tamara Berg
Berg Family Dentistry

Call Home is one of the most winsome books on prayer I've ever read. It presents prayer as a glorious opportunity and privilege, not as a loathsome or dreaded burden. The author suggests that prayer should be as easy, convenient, and instinctual as breathing. In fact, he simplifies the biblical call to "pray continually" (I Thessalonians 5:17) by showing how inviting and doable prayer really is. He contends that Jesus "wanted prayer to be as natural as calling home".

Dr. Richard Spindle
President Emeritus, MidAmerica Nazarene University

This is a refreshing book on prayer which is neither stuffy nor fluffy. Through lively humor, touching stories, and inspiring scripture, Keith's *Call Home* shares practical steps for enjoying more meaningful conversation with our heavenly Father. The included discussion questions both encouraged and challenged me, ensuring each important lesson had maximum impact.

Cheryl Crouch
Author, Teacher, General Board Church of the Nazarene

In *Call Home* Keith gives us a fresh and inspiring look at Our Lord's Prayer. It instantly took me to the Sunday afternoons when Dad, Mom, and siblings were waiting for my call. What special days those were! It also reminded me of my Dad's last words, "Son, pray for me." This book takes out the word 'discipline' to prayer and gives it the word 'pleasure.' What a great read!

Dr. Caleb Herrera
Texas-Oklahoma Latin District Church of the Nazarene

Call Home is that practical guide we all long for in deepening our relationship with God through a vibrant prayer life. Questions for reflection at the end of the chapters allow you to actively apply what is presented, creating habits that will last for a lifetime.

Dr. Tabitha Danley
Physician, SSM Health

Call Home is a fantastic encouragement to faithfully pray and connect with our Heavenly Father. I remember purchasing prepaid phone cards to call my earthly home as an out-of state college student in the 1990's. Keith reminds us that Jesus paid the price for all of us, and the miracle of prayer is available 24/7, and our Heavenly Father will never send our call straight to voicemail!

Dr. Melanie Emerson
Emerson Dentistry

Over the many years we have ministered together, Keith has been an encourager and a gifted leader. I read his book Live*Last* which has been a true inspiration to my ministry. When he informed me of a new book he was writing, I knew it would be truly inspired by his passion. He is a man of prayer, and his life has always reflected his connection with the leading of the Spirit. I recommend reading this book because it comes from the heart of a faithful leader/servant. In today's educated world comes a book from a man who is not only strong in his education but also leads with his heart.

We need leaders like Keith writing books about their walk with God. Place this book in your library and recommend it to your friends and family. You will not be disappointed!

Dr. Keven Wentworth
N/E Texas District Church of the Nazarene

In *Call Home*, Keith uses his storytelling superpower combined with scriptural truths to build a framework from The Lord's Prayer that will help you recapture a vibrant communion with the Father.

Jerolyn Bogear
Executive Coach, Leadership Trainer, Speaker & Author

Call Home not only reminds us of the power of prayer but how deep, intimate prayers put us in contact with and draw us close to the heart of our almighty God, that longs to hear from us. A book with an excellent message for the times we are living in.

Toni Miller
Board Director, President, and CFO at HerdX Inc.

Do I really need another book on prayer? The answer is no. Or, at least, I thought that was the answer until I encountered Keith's *Call Home*. Wow! I do need another book on prayer, and this is it! Read this book and live it - you will be blessed.

John deSteiguer, J.D.
President, Oklahoma Christian University

LUKE 11:1

KEITH NEWMAN

Copyright © 2023 Keith Newman

Published by Dust Jacket Press
Call Home / Keith Newman

ISBN: 978-1-953285-41-6

All rights reserved. No portion of this publication may be reproduced, stored in a retrieval system, or transmitted in any form or by any means, except for brief quotations in printed reviews, without prior permission of Keith Newman. Requests may be submitted by email to ***knewman@snu.edu***.

Dust Jacket Press
P. O. Box 721243
Oklahoma City, OK 73172
www.dustjacket.com

Scripture quotations not otherwise designated are from the Holy Bible, New International Version®, NIV® Copyright ©1973, 1978, 1984, 2011 by Biblica, Inc.® Used by permission. All rights reserved worldwide.

Permission to quote from the following versions of the Bible is acknowledged with appreciation:
The Holy Bible, English Standard Version (ESV). ESV®. Text Edition: 2016. Copyright © 2001 by Crossway Bibles, a publishing ministry of Good News Publishers.

The Message (MSG). Copyright © 1993, 1994, 1995, 1996, 2000, 2001, 2002 by Eugene H. Peterson.
New American Standard Bible (NASB). Copyright © 1960, 1962, 1963, 1968, 1971, 1972, 1973, 1975, 1977, 1995 by The Lockman Foundation

New King James Version® (NKJV). Copyright © 1982 by Thomas Nelson. Used by permission. All rights reserved.

New Living Translation (NLT). Holy Bible, New Living Translation, copyright © 1996, 2004, 2015 by Tyndale House Foundation. Used by permission of Tyndale House Publishers, Inc., Carol Stream, Illinois 60188. All rights reserved.

Scripture quotations marked KJV are from the King James Version of the Bible.

The bold format within various Scripture quotes is not part of the original quoted material and is used solely by the author for emphasis.

Dust Jacket logos are registered trademarks of Dust Jacket Press, Inc.

Cover & interior design by D. E. West / ZAQ Designs - www.zaqdesigns.com with
        Dust Jacket Creative Services

Printed in the United States of America

DEDICATION

To my children, Andy and Alana -
May you always want to call home.

CONTENTS

Foreword xiii

Introduction xv

1 Where Do I Start? 1
2 Why Don't We Call God by His Name? 17
3 Can I Really Trust God? 33
4 What Are You Going to Do with
   What You've Been Given? 51
5 When Does the Party Start? 69
6 Where Do You Choose to Stand? 83
7 Who Gets the Last Word? 101
8 What's Next? – Conclusion 113

About the Author 125

FOREWORD

I just finished reading Calling Home. My response can be summed up with one word: WOW!

I wish I had this book to read and learn from years ago.

I wanted to grow in my relationship with God. Approaching an elder of the church, I asked him what I needed to do to grow. His response was, "Go and pray!"

I waited for further instructions.

When no response came, I asked, "Is there anything else you can tell me?"

"No, just go and pray."

Awkwardly, I left him feeling confused.

I had heard about prayer. I knew I was supposed to pray. But my understanding of praying as a new follower of Jesus Christ was practically "nil." Being Chinese by descent, I grew up learning about praying to the ancestral spirits. If I did so, they would take good care of me. If I didn't, they could wreak havoc in my life. Therefore, I prayed out of fear. I didn't want bad things to happen to me.

Over the years, wonderful mentors have helped me to understand what the Bible teaches about prayer and how to pray. Because of this, I no longer pray out of fear but out of love for God.

Dr. Keith's *Call Home* is one of the best books I have read on prayer. It is inspirational, practical, motivational, and engaging. The theological insights he presents are powerful.

His words encouraged me to want to spend more time connecting with the One who loves me.

Many have a distorted view of God. They see Him as being distant, uncaring, and even harsh. At the start of his book, Keith wants us to know who the One we pray to is. Keith introduces us to God, the Father, who loves and cares for us. Then, gleaning truths from the Lord's Prayer, Keith helps us to have a deeper understanding and appreciation of prayer.

Keith practices what he writes about. For a few years he and I served at a university together. He was Chancellor, and I was Dean of the Chapel. He and I would regularly meet to share requests and then pray together. The first time we met to join our prayers together, I left his office thinking, "This man knows how to pray!"

Call Home motivates us to pray.

Keith's book deeply stirred my heart!

Jim "Umfundisi" Lo
Campus Pastor-Intercessor/ Professor,
Indiana Wesleyan University
Prayer Coordinator-
Crossroads District of The Wesleyan Church,
Anderson, Indiana

INTRODUCTION

What's your first memory of prayer? Mine is a memorized prayer that we often prayed at bedtime. Some believe the origins can be traced to Joseph Addison's essay in the March 8, 1711, publication of *The Spectator,* but the version of the prayer we prayed at our home can be traced back to the *New England Primer.*

> Now I lay me down to sleep
> I pray the Lord my soul to keep
> If I should die before I wake
> I pray the Lord my soul to take.

Looking back now it seems like it should have been a scary prayer, dying in your sleep, soul snatching in the night, but my memories of those words are all positive. There was comfort in the consistency of this nightly routine.

Though we prayed for meals, and I am certain I heard prayers in Sunday School classes and church, prayer did not become an important part of my life for many years. As I reflect on my teenage years, I wish I had discovered the beauty and the power of praying often and praying big. Alas, I did not. I'm certain that I prayed selfish prayers and fearful prayers. Though I grew up in a church that prayed often, and

I was blessed with pastors and Sunday School teachers who taught about prayer and modeled prayer for me, my prayer life could best be described as pitiful and anemic.

Along the way I had some snapshot memories about prayer that are forever embedded in my mind and heart. One was the sight of my best friend's father kneeling beside his bed in prayer with an open Bible before him. Those moments were not on display for me or anyone else to see, but their modest home featured one bathroom, and on more than one occasion I caught a glimpse of this hard-working, self-employed carpenter starting his day in prayer as I made my way to the bathroom. His voice was the loudest when we read responsively in church, and he sang hymns with an unmatched enthusiasm during worship services. Though I did not fully comprehend the significance as a teenager, I have grown to understand the powerful connection between starting your day in prayer and God's Word and a life of service in your corner of the world.

Another powerful moment for me was the voice of an elderly woman praying in the darkened youth room at my local church. By this point, I was a young police officer serving as a volunteer youth pastor. I was walking through the room that had once been the sanctuary of the church. Our youth group had inherited the space when a new sanctuary was created. The pews had been removed, but the altars remained. As I slipped through this space on the way to my office, I heard a voice that I recognized. This sweet lady worked part-time in the kitchen at the church's daycare center. She was viewed as a saint by all who knew her. I tip-toed through the room so as not to disturb her, but I stopped and listened when I heard my name. No, she didn't know and never knew I was eavesdropping on her prayer, but I heard her asking God to keep me safe on the streets of Houston and use me to minister to a group of teenagers who gathered several times a week in this space. Though I write now about an experience that happened four decades ago, the passion and power by which this godly woman prayed remain with me. Again, my prayer life was puny compared to hers, but God was planting seeds.

And that's what I hope this book might do for you. Wherever you are on your journey with God, and we are all on a journey, I pray this book will encourage you to go deeper, to find a time each day to hear God's voice and make your requests known to Him.

Years ago I was inspired by a television commercial advertising a motorcycle. Two young men are shown riding motorcycles on a highway and a sign appears welcoming them to Alaska. The next scene shows them pulling into the first place where there is a phone booth. Are you old enough to remember phone booths? One of the guys makes the phone call, and the only words in the commercial were these: "**Hey Mom, We Made It!**" My best friend and I dreamed of reliving that commercial. We were going to buy motorcycles and ride from Houston, Texas, to somewhere just inside the Alaskan border and make that phone call back home. We were crazy enough to dream about it but not crazy enough to do it.

The beauty of that commercial was the phone call back home. Here's a public service announcement: If your parents are still living, call home. There is something special about calling home. It's not the same as being there, but it helps you feel a little bit more connected to what is going on back home.

    I believe that is what happens when we PRAY. We are calling home. If the Bible is true, and I believe it is, then we are going to spend far more time in heaven than we are here on earth. True? If you are reading this book, then you haven't crossed over - you are still here - but you have the opportunity and great privilege to CALL HOME.

CALL HOME • LUKE 11:1

Where Do I Start?

"Our Father in heaven"

*"Take the first step in faith.
You don't have to see the whole staircase,
just take the first step."*
Martin Luther King, Jr.

Getting started in prayer is as simple as having a conversation with a friend. Almighty God invites us to talk to Him anytime, day or night, 24 hours a day and 365 days a year. Our prayers can be as short as one word. Help or thanks are great short prayers, and God is not interested in carefully selected words or cleverly crafted petitions. Mostly, I believe, He wants to spend time with us. Saint Teresa of Avila said it so well:

"Prayer, in my opinion, is nothing else than an intimate sharing between friends; it means taking time to be alone with him who we know loves us."

I gained a new understanding about the significance of this time with God in a most unusual place. For the last few years, our granddaughter comes to town for what I call Camp GiGi. Camp GiGi is a non-stop series of adventures that I may be getting too old for. We enjoyed trips to the zoo and science museum, bikes and hikes, horseback riding, and this year we visited a waterpark. My favorite part of the waterpark was the lazy river. Our granddaughter's favorite experience was a crazy winding, twisting, pitch-dark tunnel that spins you all around and generally increases your prayer life! I have this picture on my phone that Carolyn took of Avery and me. It shows us at the end of the ride, the only time we came out facing forward. Since she was too young to ride it by herself, but it was her favorite, we had to ride it together over and over and over again. While GiGI plans these adventures, she depends on Pop to handle all of the scary experiences. Now aside from the fear factor of this one particular slide, there was the fatigue factor of climbing up the stairs about four stories. Did I mention that we did this over and over again? On our ninth or tenth trip, we found ourselves waiting until the tube had been cleared and we were released to get started. My granddaughter looked into my eyes and said, "Pop, don't you just love this?" And I told her I did. I loved being with her and most importantly, I love her, and I don't want her to ever doubt that for even a moment. Her perspective on that moment was different, I am sure. She loved the twists and turns, the water in her face, and maybe at some level, knowing that Pop would do his best to keep her safe. The experience was shared. The perspective was different.

I got what I believe was God's perspective in a whole different way as a result of that waterslide experience. You see, I've always thought about how I felt and what I got out of spending time in stillness with God. But in that moment, I thought about the love and the joy that God has in that moment; the kind of love and joy that I experienced on a crazy waterslide with a little girl named Avery.

At the very heart of prayer is a relationship, our relationship with God. If you want to grow your relationship with God: PRAY. Prayer feeds our faith, strengthens our core, helps us heal from past hurts, and prepares us for what is coming our way: today and tomorrow.

The disciples of Jesus were in relationship with Him, and they did what great leaders do: they asked questions and they paid attention. Jesus had modeled for the disciples the importance of prayer. In quiet places after some of the busiest days, these men had watched Jesus slip away and spend time in prayer. One of the disciples, interesting to me that we do not know which one, asked for instruction. His request was recorded in Luke's gospel.

> ***One day Jesus was praying in a certain place.***
> ***When he finished, one of his disciples said to***
> ***him, "Lord, teach us to pray..."***
> ***Luke 11:1***

Jesus responded with a condensed version of what we know as the Lord's Prayer, a guide for the disciples and for us about how we might organize our thoughts in prayer. Matthew, the tax collector, gives us a longer version than Luke, the physician. We find this most famous of all prayers in Matthew chapter 6 as a portion of Jesus' Sermon on the Mount in chapter 6.

We know it as the Lord's Prayer. In the King James Version, it is sixty-six words. It can be repeated in less than a minute. Lots of people who know little or nothing about Scripture know the Lord's Prayer. Next to the 23rd Psalm, it is probably the most familiar of all passages of Scripture.

I love what Henry Ward Beecher said about the Lord's Prayer:

> **I used to think the Lord's Prayer was a short prayer; but as I live longer and see more of life, I begin to believe there is no such thing as getting through it. If a man, in praying that prayer, were to be stopped by every word until he had thoroughly prayed it, it would take him a lifetime.**

Lots of truth from those mid-19th century words. Many of us have memorized the Lord's Prayer and recited it out loud or silently, in front of a group or while drifting off to sleep. But there can be a problem as familiarity may blind us to the real message. My hope in writing this book is to have you take a fresh look at a prayer that was never intended to become mechanical. Jesus didn't teach His disciples this prayer to be used as some kind of packaged devotional or a *Get Out of Jail Free Card*. He wants it to be a Model. Jesus wants to communicate to us the joy of calling home in prayer.

I confess to you that I understand prayer about as well as I understand how cell phones work. It makes no sense at all to me that I can punch a few buttons or say a few words and instantly be connected with someone on the other side of the world. But my lack of understanding does not prevent me from using a phone, nor does it prevent me from praying.

Jesus starts with **four very powerful, very descriptive words**. Don't miss the significance of even one of them.

"Our Father in heaven..."

Several times I have led small group settings where I have distributed paper and pencils and asked the individuals present to draw a picture of God. This is one of my favorite things to do. It works from the youngest to the oldest. I've asked small children to draw a picture of God, I've asked Senior Adults to do the same, and all ages in between. The results are fascinating, especially as they begin to share their thoughts behind the picture. You can learn much about their concept of God.

Jesus, in these first few words of this prayer, was offering a completely new image of God to his listeners. Read the Old Testament and you will find that God was almost always referred to as YAHWEH, and the name was rarely spoken because of the respect and reverence associated with the name. His name was the original *shock and awe* message. Only SEVEN times in the Old Testament was God referred to as Father;

and those references were indirect and rather remote. Jesus comes along and casts off all restraint. More than 200 times in the Gospels, Jesus refers to God as Father. In His very first recorded words, Jesus explained to His parents where He was when they thought He was lost by saying:

> *"Didn't you know I had to*
> *be in my Father's house?"*
> *Luke 2:49 (NIV)*

An accident? I don't think so. Jesus understood that your image of God would have a major impact on your willingness and eagerness to CALL HOME.

I heard a radio report once about something that was going on in Afghanistan. There was a group of militant Muslims that were destroying television sets. The report said that they were doing it because television was keeping people from praying like they needed to be praying. They believed their elimination of television sets would right this wrong. While television can be a distraction, the world is filled with a host of amusements that diminish our prayer time. It seems to me that it really boils down to a couple of questions:

Are You DRAWN or DRIVEN to Pray?
Is it your First INSTINCT or Last RESORT?

I'm guessing your answers are related directly to your understanding of who God really is and how well you know Him and are aware of His work in your life. Jesus didn't teach the disciples the Lord's Prayer to drive them to pray, and He sure never intended prayer to be a last resort. He wanted prayer to be as natural as calling home.

Calling home is all about a relationship. We are naturally drawn to talk to people with whom we have a great connection. While a few of us are excited about talking to strangers (someone new to hear our stories), most people save their communication, especially about personal things, for those who know them best and they count as friends or family.

It is difficult for us to understand the significance of calling God "Our Father" when Jesus spoke these words in the model prayer. It was nothing short of revolutionary. What is a common practice for so many today was unheard of in Jesus' day. The word for Father is the word "Abba" – it was an everyday word, completely common. It can easily be translated as "DAD." It was a term of endearment. **No Jew would have ever dared to address God in this manner. But Jesus did every time He prayed, with one notable exception, when He was hanging on the cross:**

> *"My God, my God,*
> *why have you forsaken me?"*
> *Matthew 27:46*

It had been God's plan all along. Look at these verses from the prophets Jeremiah and Malachi:

> ***God said, "How gladly would I treat you like***
> ***sons and give you a desirable land, the most***
> ***beautiful inheritance of any nation.***
> ***I thought you would call me 'Father'***
> ***and not turn away from following me."***
> ***Jeremiah 3:19***

> *"Have we not all one Father?*
> *Did not one God create us?"*
> *Malachi 2:10*

Those two words: "Our Father," remind us that we are welcomed by God into His Kingdom. But the significance of those words only becomes real when we are adopted into His family through the forgiveness of our sins. The Bible says we become Joint Heirs with Jesus Christ. That means we are entitled to all the rights, privileges, and responsibilities of being called a Son or Daughter of God.

I watched with great interest the interview of Rusty Weston's father many years ago. Weston was the man convicted of killing the two Capitol Police Officers. Our church had teenagers and their sponsors in Washington D.C. at the time of the shooting and having just recently stood in the area where the shooting took place, I watched and read the news reports with great interest. The television interview with Weston's dad was painful to watch. You could tell that he was stricken with grief for the families of the slain officers and for his own son. It was apparent from the interview that this dad and mom had suffered with their son as he had struggled with mental illness. For me, the most poignant moment came when the interviewer asked Mr. Weston what he planned to say to him when he got to see him. His response was immediate, he said:

"I'm going to tell him that I love him."

And I thought to myself: That's a dad! Had their son embarrassed and humiliated them? Absolutely! But he was going to tell him that he loved him.

Jesus wanted everyone listening that day and this day to know that they have a Father in heaven that loves them and He is approachable. I know that I write to many people who don't have much of a concept of a dad. It may be because of neglect or abuse or even absence. At my own house growing up, it was absence. I was raised by a mom who attempted to be both father and mother to her four children. I'm also well aware that there are a number of people who don't even know who their earthly father is and never will. They may struggle with the concept of Our Father in Jesus' opening words of the Lord's Prayer.

I think Jesus would say to us: Let me give you a picture of a father, a real father, and I think He would begin to tell the story that He told in Luke 15. The story is of a son that took everything his father had to offer in the way of material possessions and went out and lost it all. The son didn't have much hope in life, but he knew that there was at least the slightest chance he could go back and work as a servant on his father's farm. Instead of calling home, he made the journey home. And on his way, he was rehearsing in his mind how he was going to ask for a job. But Jesus said that while that son was still a long way off, the father, standing by the mailbox at the end of their long driveway, spotted him. That Dad began to run and when the son tried to give up his sonship and offer himself as a servant, the father didn't even seem to hear him. Max Lucado says it well:

> *"You may be willing to stop being God's child. But God is not willing to stop being your Father."*

We have two kinds of relationships in life: Horizontal… our relationship with others, and Vertical…our relationship with God.

Both are critical. Damage your horizontal relationships with others, and your vertical relationship with God will struggle. The opposite is true as well. There is great significance in the fact that Jesus didn't say pray this way: "My Father in heaven." Jesus knew that both of these relationships are critical, and He addresses both with that little word "OUR." You see, we are in this together. You and I have to get along because we are a part of the same family.

Growing up, my kids liked to argue at our house about whose DAD I am. There were moments when you could just about incite a riot with my daughter over this issue. But she came to realize that she had to share me with her brother. She didn't like it, but she has come to realize it.

Jesus talked about the relationship between the concept of an earthly dad and a heavenly dad.

> *"If you then, though you are evil, know how to give good gifts to your children, how much more will your Father in heaven give the Holy Spirit to those who ask Him!"*
> **Luke 11:13**

Your dad, my dad, wants to do incredible, unbelievable things in our lives, and it starts by understanding we have the privilege of a personal relationship with Him. These first few words of the prayer tell us not only about our relationships but also the requirements or responsibilities of a father. Father is not simply a title or a role, the relationship leads to a lifetime of accountability with your children, or at least it should.

I remember trying to fulfill some of those father responsibilities a number of years ago. My son, a future biologist, needed distilled water for his aquarium. I don't understand it all, but something about Ph balance in the water. Seems like tap water would be fine to me, but since I knew nothing about aquariums, I became his taxi service to and from the store to purchase the water. Not only was I the taxi service, but I soon learned that I was his bank account as well. He was broke, and the water wasn't expensive, but when you are broke, anything is expensive. So, I fulfilled some of my responsibilities as a dad by driving and paying and helping carry the water.

Understand, I'm not complaining. I knew all this when I got into this thing called being a dad. I knew that my kids would cost me money before they ever got here, and they would cost me money every day after they got here. I didn't go into this blind. I knew I would expend time and energy, and most significantly, lots of emotion in being a dad. I knew that some days would be better than others. I knew that my patience would be tried, my wallet would be emptied, and my wisdom would be challenged. But I did it anyway.

Do you see the connection? God knew all that too when He decided that He was willing to be Our Father. He knew what He was getting into. He is not surprised or shocked by how things sometimes turn out. It is part of the price you pay in being a dad.

A few pages back I shared that next to the 23rd Psalm, the Lord's Prayer is the most well-known passage of Scripture. As I thought about that, I considered the connection between the two. I'm not sure any other passage of Scripture does as well in illustrating the responsibilities of our Father. Look at this short list of responsibilities:

- Provision: *"The Lord is my Shepherd; I shall not want…"*
- Instruction: *"He makes me lie down in green pastures…"*
- Direction: *"He leads me beside still waters… He guides me in paths of righteousness for His name's sake"*
- Restoration: *"He restores my soul."*
- Protection: *"Even though I walk through the valley of the shadow of death, I will fear no evil, for you are with me; your rod and staff they comfort me."*
- Preparation: *"You prepare a table before me in the presence of my enemies. You anoint my head with oil; my cup overflows."*

- Destination: *"Surely goodness and mercy shall follow me all the days of my life, and I will dwell in the house of the Lord forever."*

Those are just a few of the many responsibilities God promises to fulfill. You know, one of the toughest things about being a dad is that no matter how hard I try, sometimes I fail. I think you could say that for most of their growing up years, my children's strength, at least in some areas, is related to my strength. Their safety and security, their standard of living, and their standing in society are directly related to my strength in those areas, and that can be both frightening and frustrating.

The good news is this, and it is true for all of us when we choose to be adopted by our Heavenly Father, our strength is not the issue. His strength is! In fact, the Bible says,

"When you are weak, then you are strong."
2 Corinthians 12:10 (NIV)

So, if I am going to call home often, how do I get started? Great question!

Jesus told us that we should all become like children if we are going to enter the Kingdom of God. It really makes a lot of sense if we consider what it means to be reliant.

And children are great at this. When they are young, they don't worry about their daily bread, enemies, or whether or not we will forgive them. They rely on us! Children are great at doing the same thing with God. I heard a great story from a young mother who was having a conversation on the phone and learned that a friend had cancer. When she hung up the phone, this mom shared with her three-year-old daughter that they needed to pray for this friend tonight when they had bedtime prayers. Her daughter, without a moment's hesitation said, "Why don't we pray now, Mommy!"

Anytime is a great time to call home! Do you remember the Friends and Family Plan, or call on weeknights after 11 p.m. for discounted rates? Those were not the good old days! In those days, the one thing I understood less than how cell phones work was all the different long-distance plans. Here is the great news for all of us. Jesus says you can call home anytime, day or night, and you get the same rate; it is free to us. You see, He paid a great price so that we could call Our Father.

> ***"Jesus said, 'I am the way, the truth, and the life. No one comes to the Father except through me. If you really knew me, you would know the Father as well...Anyone who has seen me has seen the Father...I am in the Father and the Father is in me.'"***
> ***John 14:6-7, 9, 11 (NIV)***

Calling home is admitting that you need help, that you desire a relationship, and that you believe God is listening to every word you speak and every thought you think. Calling home demonstrates a willingness to quit trying to rely on ourselves and trust that God knows what is best. Or you can do what lots of Christians try and do. Rely on yourself until you get in over your head, and then call home. Your reliance makes all the difference in how you live your life.

One of my favorite people is Dr. Larry Mills. Larry was a professor and the head of the Business Department at Southern Nazarene University. Many years ago, I heard him tell a story about growing up on a farm in a small community in Iowa. As a youngster he developed a great love for the local high school football team. Every Friday night the team was in town, his dad would drive him down to the stadium and give him the money to go to the game. His dad would sit in his old farm truck and listen to the game on the radio. Larry said that he never even thought about the fact that his dad didn't go to the games with him.

Larry could always rely on two things. His dad always gave him money for the game, and his dad was always waiting for him in the parking lot when the game was over. It wasn't until years later he discovered that most weeks, his dad was giving him the last dollar he had so that he could enjoy the game. That's a pretty powerful picture - one that has stuck with me - a dad that gave all he had.

We have a Father who gave all He had for us.

> *"For God so loved the world that He gave His one and only Son that whoever believes in Him shall not perish but have eternal life."*
> *John 3:16*

Call Home. Your Father is waiting to hear your voice.

REFLECTION QUESTIONS:

1. What's your picture of God? Draw or describe.

2. Why do you think Jesus made prayer a priority while on earth?

3. Who modeled prayer for you?

4. Who are you modeling prayer for?

5. Review the list of responsibilities in Psalm 23; which one is most needed in your life right now? Tell your Father.

6. Is prayer your first instinct or last resort or somewhere in between?

Why Don't We Call God by His Name?

"hallowed be your name"

*"Never let the brand name on your shoes
be more important than the One
who is guiding your footsteps."*
Unknown

Bobby, lost in thought, was tracing designs in his mashed potatoes with a fork. Suddenly he interjected a serious question into his parents' conversation. "Why don't we call God by his name?" he asked. His parents were puzzled. "What do you mean, dear?" his mother asked. "I mean, why don't we call God by his name?" he repeated. "I don't understand," said his mother. "Well," explained Bobby, "in church, we always say 'Hallowed be thy name,' and then we never call Him that."

Little Bobby has a pretty good question. People have all sorts of names for God. Many of those names could be described as anything but Hallowed. What was Jesus meaning when He gave instructions about prayer, saying, "When you pray, say, Our Father in heaven….?"

"hallowed be your name"

Hallowed is not a word we commonly use. It comes from the Greek word "HAGIO" which is also the word for holy. When we pray, "Hallowed be your name," we are saying, "Let your name be holy on earth as it is in heaven." The word holy implies to be separated from everything else. Jesus sends the strong message here in the opening words of this most famous communication with God that prayer is not something we should approach lightly. When we pray the way Jesus describes, we set God apart in our thinking and feeling. We are treating Him with all the respect and honor that is due Him.

When I was about 13 years old, I went to Traffic Court with a friend of mine. My buddy had received three citations for riding his minibike on a public street. I sat in the back of the courtroom on a wooden bench and listened as the bailiff introduced the judge and asked everyone present to rise. We remained standing until the judge took his place and then we were seated and waited until the court clerk called my friend's name. I was so nervous for my friend. He walked to the front of the courtroom and stood before the judge.

Wearing his Sunday best, he answered the judge's questions with a "Yes Sir" and "No Sir." My friend, who was quite a character, was all business. I remember thinking at the time, I'm glad this isn't me. I had no idea at that time that I would spend many hours in a variety of courtrooms as an adult, for I would serve as a Houston police officer and detective. We refer to courthouses as being hallowed. It is no accident that judges are seated in an elevated position, completely separate from everyone else in the courtroom. On that night in court with my buddy, I learned something about hallowed places. When we find ourselves in a hallowed place, we need a whole different demeanor and an attitude of reverence and respect.

Now don't take what I'm writing the wrong way. I don't think Jesus was at all saying you need to be afraid when you approach God. I don't want you to receive a message that praying is like standing before a Judge. Make no mistake about it, the Bible tells us that there will be a day when every knee will bow and tongue confess that Jesus Christ is Lord. But the issue for Jesus, as He taught us how we should pray, was not to make us fearful. Earlier in this book, we explored the **relationship** that was demonstrated when Jesus chose the words, OUR FATHER, as the way He started the prayer. Those words had never been used before in praying to God. Jesus wanted us to know that as children of God, we have a Father, a dad, who is approachable. A Father that continually seeks us and is anxious for us to find Him.

Here is the question I believe this portion of the prayer is asking:

What place do we give God in our lives?

The late A.W. Tozer wrote at great length about the life of the modern church. He maintained that the **church's greatest loss today was the loss of reverence for God Himself. It was his firm conviction that God would honor any group of believers who honored Him.** What place do you give your Heavenly Father in your life? Is He more than just the man upstairs? the Big Guy in the Sky? Have you set Him apart as Lord? Do you approach prayer with a Reverence reserved for only Him?

There are three primary names of God in the Old Testament:

- **Elohim – God the Mighty Creator.**
- **Yahweh – The Lord who is the Covenant-Keeping One.**
- **Adonai – Master or Lord.**

In Jesus' time, the Jews so reverenced the name of God that they would not say the sacred name Yahweh because it was so holy. They took the consonants out of the name Yahweh and the vowels out of the name **Adonai**, put them together, and formed a new word that King James writers translated **JEHOVAH**. When Jewish scholars copied the Scriptures, they selected a new pen with which to write God's name so they would not dishonor God by writing His name with a pen that had been used to write other words. After using the new pen to write God's name, they broke it so it could never be used again.

Now that sounds rather silly to us, but God's name was very serious to them. While their practice could be considered very legalistic, I'm afraid we often approach God in a very lazy manner. Maybe it is my imagination (I don't think so), but it seems as if there has been a persistent and consistent loss of reverence for all things sacred over the past half-century. Honor and respect seem to have lost their importance and the multiple media messages continue to contribute to the slide. In the midst of what feels like an absence of reverence for all things sacred, I believe there is a huge opportunity for devoted followers of Jesus. We can model a different way. If the world gets darker, our light will shine brighter, but it takes intentionality. It is not a longing for the old ways but a choice to take the higher way.

If I could draw in your Bible, I think I would want to put a big RED STOP SIGN immediately following the words, "Hallowed be your Name." (I've done this in my Bible). Because that is exactly what Jesus is wanting us to do; to stop, to set apart, to see God in His holiness, and to revere Him before we really get started in prayer. God is holy. We are called to be holy. The disciple who struggled the most to not say everything he thought quoted Leviticus 11:44 when he wrote these words…

> *"But just as He who called you is holy,*
> *so be holy in all you do; for it is written:*
> *'Be holy because I am holy.'"*
> *1 Peter 1:15-16*

Have you been to any Hallowed Places? I bet you have! Hospital maternity wards are hallowed places to me. I have stood and held brand-new babies in the midst of Neonatal Intensive Care Units. Tiny fingers with even tinier fingernails, skin softer than anything in the world, babies that gave me a great big yawn and I could see tiny tonsils. What an incredible sight! What a hallowed place!

Snowcapped mountains with water running down the side into streams, blue skies, and an eagle with wings spread riding the air currents…that is a hallowed place for me.

Worship services when God's presence is so very real and there really aren't any words that need to be said. That's a hallowed place.

Even worship rehearsals and choir practices can be hallowed places. I'll never forget being in a church business meeting and leaving to get a cup of coffee from the kitchen. I stood and heard nearby the sounds of a worship team rehearsing, and before I knew it, I found myself drawn to stand outside the door and listen. It was a hallowed place and a hallowed moment.

When we choose to hallow God's name, I think it leads us to be silent and still, two very challenging assignments in our noisy worlds with music and media at our fingertips and, more often than not, in our ears.

Jesus walked the streets of this earth, and I think He knew what a great temptation it is for all of us to rush into prayer. We want to get right to the good stuff. Or maybe I'm the only one tempted to do that. I've got my list of people and places and things I need to pray about, and often the compulsion to pray comes when things are going well. And

I know that I need to praise God and thank Him, but there is still this great temptation to rush through that and get to the heart of the matter.

And then Jesus puts up this Stop Sign and I don't think He wants us to roll through it. He wants us to come to a complete stop and not just look both ways but stop and look up. And then, when we see God, we will be silent and still.

Honoring God's Name can create some sense of order in our lives.

Your name is more than just your name. It represents more than just the family you were born into and the name that your parents chose for you. It implies much more. God's name reveals His title, His person, His power, His authority, His character, and His reputation.

When we pray, "Hallowed be Your Name," we are honoring the holiness of God. And the holiness of God is like a tent pole holding up everything. When it is no longer there, or when people no longer respect and revere it, then there is no longer reverence for anything. Look around, society is reaping what has been sown.

Back in the 1950s, a young woman in West Germany scrawled across a cathedral door in her town the words, "Elvis Presley – My God." At the time, people laughed. A girl from Germany worshipping a rock and roll star from America. But her words could have been a sign of what was to come, for today, we have people worshipping anything and everything, but mostly themselves. I ask again: Have you noticed that there is very little that is reverenced anymore? You see when you take the center tent pole down, everything else comes down as well.

The good news is that you and I can raise that tent pole in our lives. We can hallow the name of the Father. We can stop and honor the name and, in doing so, bring order back into what, at times, can be a chaotic world.

Remember the Scripture...

"Be still and know that I am God."
Psalm 46:10

The people that day stood in awe and wonder at how God had saved them from certain destruction. There were no words on their lips, only stillness and silence. You and I desperately need those times beside still waters and in green pastures. Those are the moments when God can really reveal to us who He is.

I think a man in the Old Testament learned that lesson. His name was Job. You probably remember his story. Enemies had slaughtered his cattle, lightning had destroyed his sheep, and strong winds had left his children buried in the rubble of what once was a house. And that all happened on the first day. Before the insurance claims adjuster could get out to inspect, Job came down with leprosy and boils covered his body. His wife told him just to curse God and die. She understood something about what happened when you cursed God; however, she didn't have a great picture of what it means to Hallow His Name. Job had four friends that came to visit him, and they began to try and convince him that his problem was sin, and if he would just confess his sin, then things might get better. They all gave their theological treatises and in between theirs, Job gave his. Nobody was still, nobody was silent for 23 chapters! Then Job decided to speak, he gives us another 6 chapters. He tells us all about God. In fact, you could get the impression that Job knew more about God than God knew about Himself. Thirty-seven chapters go by before God decides to speak. Chapter thirty-eight starts with these words: "**Then the Lord answered Job!**" Listen to some of what God had to say:

> *"Where were you when I laid the earth's foundation?*
> *Tell me, if you understand.*
> *Who marked off its dimensions? Surely you know!*
> *Who stretched a measuring line across it?*
> *On what were its footings set,*
> *or who laid its cornerstone—*
> *while the morning stars sang together*
> *and all the angels shouted for joy?*
> *Who shut up the sea behind doors*
> *when it burst forth from the womb,*
> *when I made the clouds its garment*
> *and wrapped it in thick darkness,*
> *when I fixed limits for it*
> *and set its doors and bars in place,*
> *when I said, 'This far you may come and no farther;*
> *here is where your proud waves halt'*
> *Have you ever given orders to the morning,*
> *or shown the dawn its place,"*

Job 38:4-12

You may be like Job and think you have it all figured out, or maybe you just have lots of questions. Jesus says, take time to stop and honor the Father's Name, be still, be silent, and let order come back into your life.

Job got the message. Chapter 40, verse 4 says this about Job's response:

> *"I am not worthy; I cannot answer you anything, so I will put my hand over my mouth."*

I confess to you that sometimes, far too often, I need to just put my hand over my mouth, be still, be silent, and know that God is God. That's what happens when we really hallow His Name.

When we choose to hallow God's Name, hope rises, and holiness is pursued. We are running towards God. If you will study the Bible closely, you will see that the words Holy and Hope go together. Where you see one, you will see the other, either in the same verse or at least close by. There is a great connection between the two. Jesus gives us the Lord's Prayer as a model prayer in the midst of the Sermon on the Mount. The Sermon on the Mount is many things, but I think you could rightfully say that it is a message about living a holy life in an unholy world. When we pray to a holy God and see Him in all His righteousness, like Isaiah in the temple, we will hear His call to holiness.

Holiness is the hope of our world. Our world needs people who will raise the tent pole, hallowing God's Name in their own life, in the life of their family, their church, and their world. We are to be more than peace lovers or peacekeepers. We are to be peacemakers, taking righteousness into our world.

When we think about righteousness, I am reminded that we can honor or dishonor our family name. Our son had a friend that lived in the neighborhood next to ours. One afternoon this friend arrived at our house prior to our son, Andy, arriving home. Brandon was one of those friends who was in and out of our house several times a week, he ate dinner with us on a fairly regular basis, he felt at home at our house, and we felt like he was a part of the family. While I didn't know Brandon well at the time, I knew that he was a servant. When he was at our house, he brought honor to his family's name. I'm not sure what he was like at home, but I know what he was like with us. On this particular day, when he arrived early, instead of just sitting around watching television waiting for Andy to arrive, he jumped right in without being asked and helped me make a bed with freshly laundered sheets. If you want to impress your friend's parents, jump in and help with household chores. Now this wasn't an Eddie Haskell (*Leave it to Beaver* reference for the younger generation) kind of a thing. Brandon liked to help. The next day his dad happened to call the house and I commended him for having such a fine son. You see, he had brought honor to his family's name.

By extension, our name honors or dishonors God's name because when we choose to follow Christ, we become the bearer of His name. As a Christian, I carry the name of Christ everywhere I go. I heard two sports talk show hosts discuss the name of a prominent football coach in the National Football League. They were laughing about the fact that he doesn't allow cursing and swearing in training camp, a tribute they say to his newfound Christian faith. What seemed to bother these guys the most was not the ban on cursing and swearing but the fact that this same coach admitted that gambling was still one of his favorite things to do. These worldly guys had measured this football coach's Christianity up to his lifestyle, and he had failed the test as a hypocrite in their eyes.

Solomon understood the value of a good name. He wrote…

> ***"A good name is more desirable than***
> ***great riches; to be esteemed is better***
> ***than silver or gold."***
> ***Proverbs 22:1***

When I lived in Indiana, I had the chance to spend some time with Bill Gaither - what an amazing and gifted influencer for the cause of Christ. Gaither tells a story about the value of a good name in his book *I Almost Missed the Sunset*. He writes that he and his wife Gloria had been married for a couple of years and were both teaching school in Alexandria, Indiana, where he had grown up. They wanted to buy a piece of land where they could build a house. He noticed a beautiful piece of property south of town where cattle grazed. He learned it belonged to a 92-year-old retired banker named Mr. Yule. He owned a lot of land all over the area, but the word was that he wouldn't sell any of it. He gave the same speech to everyone who inquired, "I promised the farmers they could use it for their cattle." Although retired, Mr. Yule spent a couple of hours every morning at the bank. Bill and Gloria Gaither went to visit him at the bank one morning. Here is what happened in Bill's words:

> He looked at us over the top of his bifocals. I introduced myself and told him we were interested in a piece of land. 'Not selling,' he said pleasantly. 'Promised it to a farmer for grazing.' 'I know, but we teach school here and thought maybe you'd be interested in selling to someone planning on settling in the area.' He pursed his lips and stared at me. 'What'd you say your name was?' 'Gaither, Bill Gaither.' 'Hmmm. Any relation to Grover Gaither?' 'Yes sir, he was my granddad.' Mr. Yule put down his paper and removed his glasses. 'Interesting. Grover Gaither was the best worker I ever had on my farm. Full day's work for a day's pay. So honest. What'd you say you wanted?' I told him again.

A week later, Bill Gaither owned fifteen acres for a fraction of what it was worth. He wrote that nearly 30 years later, he and his son strolled that beautiful, lush property that had once been pasture. 'Benjy,' I said. 'you've had this wonderful place to grow up through nothing that you've done but because of the good name of a great-granddad you never met.'

Now, if an earthly name can mean so much, how much more can the name of God mean?

"Hallowed be your name"…the tent pole goes up, order prevails, and the world shakes off chaos.

"Hallowed be your name," …and when it is, the soul knows its home. There is holiness…there is hope!

When we hallow God's name, there is a natural response, we worship and find ourselves willing or at least prepared to be willing. The Lord's Prayer teaches us the sovereignty of God the King, but it also teaches us that people have a free will. Adam could choose to eat of the forbidden fruit. Abraham could choose to lie. Peter could choose to deny. Judas could choose to betray. And they all chose wrong.

We choose worship!

"Worship the Lord in the beauty of holiness."
Psalm 96:9

The command is to worship God. We do that when we hallow His Name. But the choice is still ours. Some people don't worship God because of ignorance, even though their inner hearts know God. Some people don't worship because their hearts are rebellious because of sin - they are caught up in the world of Me. Some people don't worship God because they are too busy with the cares of the world. Some people have just forgotten because other things have crowded out God.

Jesus says CALL HOME, but when you do, start by slowing down. In fact, stop. Hallow the Father's Name. Worship. Let those moments of reverence prepare your heart. Willingness to take the next step will be the result. My hope, my prayer, my dream is that prayer will be so natural, so authentic, so much a part of our life that wherever we find ourselves will be a hallowed place.

Earlier in this chapter I told the story of that teenage friend of mine who had to stand before the judge in municipal court while I sat on the back row of the courtroom. What I failed to tell you was that his father was standing right beside him the whole time.

You and I have a Heavenly Father that walks with us, even through valleys. The Bible tells us that our Savior Jesus Christ is at the right hand of God even right now making intercession for us. The Word of God goes on to say that even when we don't know how to pray, the Holy Spirit prays for us.

I'm not sure how that makes you feel, but it makes me anxious to call home.

REFLECTION QUESTIONS:

1. How did you get your name and how has that name impacted your journey?
2. What are some "hallowed places or spaces" you've experienced?
3. When you think of holiness, what picture comes to mind?
4. Who commands your respect and why?
5. How could your prayer time be more conducive to hallowing God's Name?
6. Are there opportunities for your light to move into darkness? What's stopping you?
7. What are some ways the church could impact a disrespectful culture for the cause of Christ?

3

Can I Really Trust God?

*"your kingdom come, your will be done,
on earth as it is in heaven."*

*"Keep trusting God.
He is always in control even when your
circumstances seem out of control."*
Unknown

It was a holiday weekend back in 1979, and while the rest of the country was celebrating, Hurricane David was bearing down on the Florida coast. A group of single guys were trying to figure out how to secure their houseboat to ride out the expected storm. Of great significance to the story is that they had only owned the boat for about three months. Their preparation for the high winds and rough seas was to acquire all of the rope they could find, and they began to fasten the boat to everything they could find to tie it to - trees, docks, anything! One of the guys described the scene like a rerun from McHale's Navy. When they had used up all their rope and surveyed their work, it looked a little like a spider's web. An old timer came along and laughed at what they had done. He said:

"Boys, your only hope is to anchor deep, leave the rope slack, and pray for the best!"

Those wise words of advice from that seasoned sailor seem to fit this next portion of the Lord's Prayer. Jesus gave us a prayer that will work on sunshiny days and on stormy nights. He was concerned about where we choose to anchor our souls. He knew that life is guaranteed to bring us some storms. So regardless of the weather or the meteorological forecast, can you pray the words below?

"Your kingdom come; your will be done on earth as it is in heaven."

Can you trust God with all of your life? I know this is a personal question, and I'm not just talking about the parts of your life you are willing to release, but can you trust God with everything? I would guess that the Lord's Prayer has been prayed billions and billions of times with little thought given to what these words of surrender really mean.

I grew up a few blocks from the Atlantic Ocean and we spent quite a bit of time at the beach. One of our favorite childhood games was played on the big sand dunes that separated the beach from the highway. The game was KING of the HILL. You know the object of the game, whoever manages to stay up on top gets to claim the title, King of the Hill. The challengers attempt to dethrone the king. I hated that game! And it was because I was skinnier and scrawnier than all of my friends, and I never got to be king.

While that was just a game, in real life I've tried being King of the Hill and I'm guessing that you have too! Some of you are still King of the Hill in your life. When we believe we are King of the Hill, then we believe we determine our own destiny, arrange our own affairs, and govern our own lives. We become supreme specialists in selfish, self-centered living where all of life revolves around Me and Mine.

I guess what I'm saying is that while it is easy to pray, **"Your kingdom come, your will be done, on earth as it is in heaven,"** it must be more than words. Let me ask you some Kingdom questions. Who is your king? In the United States we live in a democracy. Most of us have never experienced what it means to live in a place governed by a king or queen. Kings and queens are sovereign, they are supreme in power and authority. There is no external control. They don't answer to anyone else. But it is important to remember that a king is not a king without a kingdom to rule over.

Jesus tells us in this Lord's Prayer that not only do we have a Father, but also, we have a King and there is a Kingdom. This portion of the prayer, **"Your kingdom come, Your will be done, on earth as it is in heaven,"** then becomes an invitation. The invitation is to choose to accept God as the sovereign ruler of our lives. That's what you are praying when you pray this portion of the prayer.

A few folks reading this book might remember a radio, and then television show called "Queen for a Day?" I have a very faint recollection of it, so I had to call some older friends and get additional information. Queen for a Day was a show that honored a particular woman. The host would begin each show by asking: "Would you like to be Queen for a Day? The audience then had the opportunity to vote after hearing each woman speak about their financial plight. An applause meter, typically louder for the more desperate situations, selected the woman who would be Queen for the Day. She was then provided a red velvet robe and a jeweled crown, and was seated on a throne and given lots of great gifts. The host of this show would always sign off by saying: "This is Jack Bailey, wishing we could make *every* woman a queen, for every single day!"

I wonder if we often treat God the same way. We let Him be King for a Day, and we may toss Him some gifts, and say some nice things, but then we want to climb back to the top of the hill and regain the throne. The Psalmist David testified….

"You are my King, and my God."
Psalm 44:4

Paul testified to Timothy….

CALL HOME • LUKE 11:1

"Now to the King eternal, immortal, invisible, the only God, be honor and glory for ever and ever. Amen."
1 Timothy 1:17

The Kingdom Question, "who is the King," is a huge issue to be resolved in the life of every believer. It is the difference between Jesus Christ being just the Savior of your life or allowing Him to be the Lord of your life. I believe how you answer that question determines whether or not your life will be a battle or a blessing!

Another Kingdom question before us is where is the Kingdom? Is it here and now or way out there in the distant future where we really don't need to consider it much? Remember that almost every time Jesus prayed, he referred to God as Father. Father was one of his favorite expressions. He had a couple of more favorite phrases: the Kingdom of God and the Kingdom of Heaven. His closest followers had a difficult time comprehending just what exactly the Kingdom was all about. Most of them were quite sure that it was an earthly empire that He would establish. The people He spoke to on the mountainside that day were weary and angry at the abuse they were enduring under the rule of the Romans. They saw Jesus as some kind of a superhero figure that was going to kick the bad guys out of the country. He would be the next King David, their hero from yesteryear. You can imagine how disappointed they were when they saw Jesus go willingly to a cross. By the way, do you remember what Jesus prayed in the Garden only hours before He went to the cross?

> *"My Father, if it is possible,*
> *may this cup be taken from me.*
> *Yet not as I will, but as you will."*
> **Matthew 26:39**

The Lord's Prayer was not something Jesus offered as a model to be prayed mechanically. It was a prayer that would come alive in the lives of all disciples so that when the storms of life come, you can anchor deep, leave the rope slack, and pray for the best. So where is the kingdom? Bible scholars and theologians have argued about this for years. Some make a distinction between the Kingdom of God and the Kingdom of Heaven. Others see the Kingdom of Heaven as some divine dynasty that is to be established on earth. Still, others see the kingdom of God as the social activity and outreach of the Church during this time in human history. Jesus Himself gave us some great insight into the Kingdom of God. Look at these words from Luke.

> *"The Kingdom of God does not come visibly,*
> *now will people say, 'Here it is,' or 'There it is,'*
> *because the kingdom of God is within you."*
> **Luke 17:20-21**

You and I have a throne. In fact, Paul told us that our bodies are the temple of God and the Holy Spirit dwells within us. The significance of all that is this:

When I pray, *"Your kingdom come, your will be done..."* I am willing to relinquish the rule of my own affairs, to abstain from making my own decisions in order to allow God, by His indwelling Spirit, to decide for me what I should do. That brings us to the next kingdom question, does God have a personal plan for my life? You may have heard someone say: God has a wonderful plan for your life. And I am tempted to add, so does everyone else!

God does have a wonderful plan for your life, and He has for each and every life, if we find it and follow it. One of my favorite representations of this concept is found in Peter's sermon in Acts where he reminds his listeners of what God did in David's life.

> *"David served God's purpose in his own generation, then he died..."*
> *Acts 13:36 (CEB)*

Another translation says,

> *"David carried out God's purpose while he lived. Then he died."*
> *(NIRV)*

The point being: God had a plan for David's life and David lived out that plan. Wouldn't it be great if that could be said about you and me? Remember this verse?

> *"All the days ordained for me were written in your book before one of them came to be."*
> *Psalm 139:16*

We were created uniquely different, not one of us with the same fingerprints, and yet there is a different plan for every one of us. The issue is whether it will be God's will or my will. What is God's will? Well, as a noun, it could be described as a blueprint for our lives. A few years ago, I had the opportunity to be a part of two construction projects. I was not building anything, but I was responsible for leading a congregation through these projects. About once a day, I would go out to visit the construction office. They did not need my help, but it made me feel like I was more a part of it if I went out there and visited with them for 10 minutes. Every time I went, I saw blueprints. Every building has a different set of blueprints, and every person has a different plan. Blueprints are the big picture! God's will, God's plan will provide guidance and direction as you make decisions today that will determine the destiny of tomorrow.

Somewhere along the way I learned about the three expressions of God's will: **dictated, desired, and directed**. The dictated will of God are the laws by which God runs the universe. You don't have to make decisions about these. God has established the laws of nature like gravity and the temperature at which water will boil or freeze. These are automatic. The prophet Isaiah gives us some help with the dictated will of God.

> *"Surely as I have planned, so it will be,*
> *and as I have purposed, so it will stand."*
> *Isaiah 14:24*

The desired will of God is the perfect plan that does not always happen. God desires that we should all pray, that we should all ask for forgiveness, and that we should all be saved. Even though that is His desire, not everyone is going to do that. When you pray, **"Your will be done"** you are saying you want to see His desires accepted and embraced in this world. A verse about God's plan that sometimes goes unnoticed or under noticed are these words from Jesus:

> **"For God did not send His Son into the world to condemn the world, but to save the world through Him."**
> **John 3:17**

One expression of God's will comes in the form of commands, the directed will of God. Some of those commands we know about, some of them we are still learning about, but just as a mom or dad expects obedience from a child when they have made their directions perfectly clear, God expects the same thing from us. Nothing is quite as exciting as discovering God's plan for your life. Notice I said God's Plan. Not your mom's or your dad's plan, your brother's or sister's, your next-door neighbor's, or even your pastor's, but God's. When God makes His will clear, say, "Yes."

Many years ago, in 1989, I believe, our little family was living in a small town in Arkansas, and I found myself needing to discern God's will. We had lived in the community for about two years, and I was serving as a lead pastor, my first time with this responsibility. The church had doubled in size (still a small congregation), and we were enjoying the pace and rhythm of life after having lived in the fourth-largest city in the country for so many years. Van Buren, Arkansas, had little resemblance to Houston, Texas. It was a place where people seldom locked their doors, and I could see much of my congregation if I visited the local Walmart on a Saturday afternoon!

Out of the blue, I received a phone call with an invitation to interview to be the pastor of a church in Houston. It was the oldest of the Churches of the Nazarene in the city and I knew quite a bit about their history and current condition. Once the largest church of the denomination in the city and the "mother" of eighteen other churches that had been planted throughout the city, it had fallen on hard times and had relocated to an area of the city that was challenged from a socio-economic perspective. The church was renting a health club that had gone bankrupt and the previous buildings and property of the church were for sale, but there were no prospective buyers. The congregation had squabbled, split, and diminished. Nothing about the prospects of moving back to Houston to serve this church appeared very attractive. I had no interest in interviewing for the position as I was happy where we were living and serving, and if the truth were known, I thought my next assignment would be a better opportunity. Though not proud to admit it now, I am certain that I thought I deserved a better second church than what was being suggested in Houston.

A conversation with my wife created at least a tiny bit of openness to making the trip to Houston and meeting with the church board. She told me a story of attending a district women's retreat several months before and an experience she had following this gathering. It should be noted that she did not want to attend the retreat but felt obligated as the pastor's wife. Jeannie McCullough was the speaker at the retreat, and she spoke extensively about the power of God's Word in a person's life. She encouraged the participants to go home and do several things:

- Read a book of the Bible that was unfamiliar.
- Read in that book until you got a clear message about what you were reading.
- Write that message down in the margin of your Bible.

Carolyn never told me about the retreat until I shared with her the opportunity I had to interview for the church in Houston. At that point, she opened her Bible and turned to the book of Ezekiel, and she told me the story of the retreat. One Sunday after the retreat, during some quiet moments and in, of all places, the church nursery, she practiced what she had learned at the retreat. She found herself reading a passage in Ezekiel, she felt like God was telling her that at some point in the future (not necessarily now, but some day), our family would return to Houston. In the margin of her Bible, she had noted the date and written the word Houston. Carolyn quickly told me that she didn't know whether now was the time and she was not encouraging a return to Houston, but she felt like I needed to know of her "strange" experience.

Based on my conversation with Carolyn, I traveled to Houston and interviewed for the position. The interview went well and all but one of the board members voted in favor of extending an invitation for me to become their new pastor. I had so many mixed emotions after the conversation with their church board and my tour of the parsonage and rented church facilities. While the size of the city and the opportunity to return to our hometown where we knew so many people was attractive, the church was challenged with few resources and lots of obstacles.

A few days passed after my return to Arkansas and the church in Houston was wanting an answer about whether or not I would consider their invitation to become their next pastor. I requested a few more days to pray and make a determination and promised them an answer by the following Monday evening at the latest. After a busy weekend, I went to my office at the church on Monday morning, wondering how I would find peace about what we should do related to this invitation. The timing felt awkward as we had not been living in Arkansas for a long period of time, and it felt premature to leave our current church. There was certainly some sentimentality about returning home to a city we loved. Bottom line: I was a mess! I didn't know what to do, and I didn't want to get it wrong.

In my office that morning I was alone. The church was empty. I sat on a floral loveseat that had been Carolyn's when we got married. We had used it at home until we moved to Arkansas, and I located it in my office. As I sat there and prayed, I asked God for direction. My sense of direction from God in those moments was to do what I normally did, have my devotions. From my desk I took my devotional, *A Prayer Guide for Ministers and Servants*, published by Abingdon Press. It was a gift I had received a few years prior. Organized by weeks instead of a particular date, I found myself reading the assigned passages for the week, and when I got to the Monday reading, it was from Ezekiel. Strange, I thought, but it was not the same chapter as the passage Carolyn had read to me. In fact, I believe the two passages were 20-plus chapters apart. As I began to read the assigned reading for that Monday, I discovered that it was the exact same passage as Carolyn's, just in a different chapter and repeated twice in Ezekiel. Strange, but true. I knew at that moment we were to return to Houston. I picked up the phone and called Carolyn to tell her that we were moving back to our hometown.

Definitely strange, but I am convinced it was the right thing to do, and God knew that I needed something *different from what is usual, ordinary, or expected* if I was going to have peace about making this move. Years removed from this experience, I can testify that it was absolutely the right decision and God-ordained.

Well, that brings us to the million-dollar question that I hear a lot, how can you know God's plan? It begins by making Christ the Lord of your life, establishing Christ and Christ alone on the throne of your life, and then praying this part of the Lord's Prayer and meaning it. This third petition in the Lord's Prayer is a request that God's will be done in your life.

Notice that you are not asking God to do His will or to change His will; and you do not ask God to bless your will. You are wanting to experience His will and His will alone in your life. So, my best suggestion is to pray and here are Four Prayers about God's Plan for your life:

1. Help me to **FIND** the plan. *Psalm 143:10 "Teach me to do your will, for you are my God; may your good Spirit lead me on level ground."*

2. Help me to **UNDERSTAND** the plan. *Ephesians 5:17 "Therefore do not be foolish but understand what the Lord's will is."*

3. Help me to **SUBMIT** to the plan. *Romans 12:1-2 "Offer your bodies as living sacrifices…be transformed by the renewing of your mind. Then you will be able to test and approve what God's will is…His good, pleasing, and perfect will."*

4. Help me to **ACCOMPLISH** the plan. *Philippians 1:6 "He who began a good work in you will carry it on to completion."*

When you pray, "your will be done," it may be a prayer of yielding your will to God's will, and you may have to pray that prayer repeatedly until you really are willing to live with the results. A flight instructor can teach a student all about flying a plane, they can have hours of classroom instruction, they can watch video tapes, and they can even fly together, but there comes a time when the controls are turned completely over to the student.

You may know God has a plan for your life and understand what it means. You may have read books, studied Sunday School lessons, and heard sermons about what it means to yield your life to God, but there comes a time when you finally let God take over. That brings us to the final question…

So, what are the results of finding and following God's plan? I think I can best describe it by telling you first what it is not like. It is not like the kindergarten boy who kept standing up in class even though the teacher asked him to sit down. She tried peer pressure with him. She pointed out that everyone else was sitting down, and she asked him if he would sit down. When the little boy continued to stand, the teacher gently put her hand on his shoulder and helped him sit down. In desperation, he blurted out, "I may be sitting on the outside, but I'm standing on the inside."

Finding and following God's will is not outward submission and inward rebellion. It is when you reach the place where you experience the safety, security, and inner peace that comes from walking in God's will. Remember, Jesus said, "**the kingdom of God is within you."** Look at what Paul said,

> *"God's kingdom isn't a matter of what you put in your stomach, for goodness' sake. It's what God does with your life as He sets it right, puts it together, and completes it with joy. Your task is to single-mindedly serve Christ."*
> **Romans 14:17-18 (MSG)**

It is an inside job! While some were concerned about the externals, Paul understood that when we get the inside issues settled, the outside stuff works out fine. You see, **God's WILL becomes MY will!**

To pray, "your will be done," is a wonderful release, and there is a freedom and peace that comes from letting Jesus take the wheel. I love these guidelines about finding and doing God's will, and I hope you will find them helpful.

> **a. Does it agree with God's WORD?** If your decision conflicts with what has already been written in God's Word, don't do it. You'll be sorry. Trust me, I have stories and scars!
>
> **b. Have you been here BEFORE?** And if you have, what did God show you was His will then? If you made a mistake, don't repeat it. I wish I could tell you that I've never repeated history, bad history, in my life, but I have. God keeps bringing us back to the same place so we can learn, and for some of us, we learn the hard way.
>
> **c. Seek COUNSEL.** Solomon said, **"Plans fail for lack of counsel."** Proverbs 15:22 None of us are ever too wise to not need to seek out counsel. Find someone that is mature and Godly and ask for his or her advice. I promise there are people ready, willing, and equipped to assist you if you would humble yourself and ask.
>
> **d. BATHE it in prayer.** Find a quiet place. Make an appointment with God. Go with a determination that you are going to pray specifically for God's will in this par-

ticular situation. The old timers talked about "praying through," and I believe they were on to something. If it is not clear, stay on your knees, and keep praying and seeking. You will find it!

e. Don't ignore the OBVIOUS. God gives a great body of practical knowledge, and we shouldn't ignore it. Some things we struggle with unnecessarily. We know the answer before we ever breathe a prayer. I love the Captain Obvious commercials, and more often than we probably want to admit, we know the obvious but are trying to delay or negotiate. My advice: Don't!

f. WAIT! Sometimes circumstances and situations can change just because we wait. God solves the problem or works out a solution, and it was all because we didn't get in a hurry. So many times, when I have simply waited, circumstances changed, problems were resolved, and I would have messed it up by acting too quickly.

g. Expect PEACE. Doors will open or close and God will give you a real inner peace if you have honestly and openly prayed, "not my will, but yours."

We end where we started. Are you anchored deep? Can you pray this part of the Lord's Prayer and mean it? Have you made God more than just King for the Day? Do you want to continue to be the King of the Hill or are you tired of trying to run your own life?

Jesus has great advice for us, He simply says: **CALL HOME.**

REFLECTION QUESTIONS:

1. Spend a few moments thinking about the last storm you experienced. What was the lesson you took away from the storm?

2. Why do you think it is so hard for most of us to pray (and mean) this portion of the Lord's Prayer?

3. Is there a Bible character that you think best exemplifies living the results of a surrendered life?

4. Has finding God's personal plan for your life been a struggle or come easy for you and how has that impacted others?

5. Which of the four prayers for finding God's plan in your life is most relevant in this season?

6. Are you, like David, fulfilling God's purpose in your generation? If not, how can you get on track? Who in your circle of influence might help you? What spiritual disciplines would be especially important in these moments?

CALL HOME • LUKE 11:1

4

What Are You Going to Do with What You've Been Given?

"Give us today our daily bread."

"The world asks: What does a man own?
Christ asks: How does he use it?"
Andrew Murray

When Carolyn and I got married, one of the most unusual gifts we received was a box containing everything you needed to make homemade bread. There were cookbooks, mixes, special tools, and pans for baking bread. Carolyn wasn't nearly as excited about the gift as I was. Now I don't know how to do much more than boil water and make peanut butter and jelly sandwiches, but I love a challenge, so I set out to bake some homemade bread. And though I nearly destroyed the kitchen in the process, I got pretty good at making all sorts of bread. There is nothing quite like the smell and taste of homemade bread hot out of the oven.

Well, it wasn't long until I gave up my bread-making career. It was just too much work, and besides, you could go to the store and buy virtually every kind of bread imaginable. Buying a regular loaf of bread these days is like trying to buy a regular Bible. There are a great number of parallels between bread and the Bible. Perhaps one of them being that we take both for granted.

Jesus offers what seems to me to be a line out of place or at least random in the Lord's Prayer when He prayed...

"Give us today our daily bread."

This line appears out of place or random because it doesn't seem to fit with the magnificence of the other elements of the prayer. Bread seems kind of basic to me amid a prayer where we have recognized that we have a Father who is not only a Father but a King, and when we allow Him the throne of our life, then we discover that yes, we can trust Him. And I know what is coming up in this model prayer too! Jesus is going to talk about the big issues of forgiveness and temptation. At first glance, bread just seems out of place to me. Unless bread can represent something more than just a loaf that we think about when we hear the word bread. Could it be that bread represents resources in our life?

Think about the number of different ways that we use the word bread in our language. When we talk about the breadbasket, we are talking about a geographical location where wheat is harvested. Breadwinners represent people who are out earning a living, and we know that sometimes the word bread is used as a slang word for money.

Jesus could have prayed: "Give us today our daily fish," or "Give us today our daily potato," or "Give us today our daily broccoli" (aren't you glad He didn't pray that?). Jesus chose the word bread specifically. Maybe it is because of the characteristics of bread. Bread is about as simple and basic as it gets. In fact, can you think of anything more common than bread? Everyone in first-century Palestine and everyone reading these pages understands bread. Jesus would later take a little boy's sack lunch (John 5) with some bread and fish and feed the multitudes. That little boy had to decide that day the same thing you and I must decide each day and that is:

What are you going to do with what you've got?

Would you have donated your entire lunch? Not me, and I'm certain my daughter wouldn't have. Growing up, Alana ate like a bird, and most nights at dinner, even though she hadn't started eating what she had on her plate, she was worried about who might get seconds. Sound familiar? We are more concerned about what is out there that we might somehow get than we are with what we already have. Well, not only is bread simple, but it is also universal. A few years ago, I was in the Ukraine, which is considered the breadbasket of the former Soviet Union. The only thing that I ever had to eat that I could really identify while there was bread. And I ate lots of bread! No matter where you go in the world, you will find some type of bread. It may be in the form of a tortilla or a kind of a cracker, but bread is universal. I don't believe it was an accident that Jesus chose bread as a metaphor for our most basic needs in this prayer.

Some would interpret this portion of the Lord's Prayer simply as a request for those things that we need to sustain our physical lives. We are fortunate in this United States that the vast majority spend very little time thinking about the provisions needed daily. Instead, we spend time focused on the choices. What will I choose to eat today? Which pair of shoes match this outfit? Some people even make choices about which car they are going to drive today. We are self-sufficient, and as a result, possibly the easiest part of the Lord's Prayer to pray is: "Give us today our daily bread." But we can look at this prayer another way, on a higher plane, with a request for spiritual strength to do God's will. Jesus chose bread to represent His body in the celebration of the Lord's Supper. So, remember the context as Jesus had just prayed: "Your kingdom come, Your will be done, on earth as it is in heaven." Could the message be if you are going to be about kingdom business, then you need both physical and spiritual strength?

The picture beautifully illustrates the message Jesus is offering in teaching His disciples (and us) about prayer. Our society and even the church tends to compartmentalize what we do. We want to separate the spiritual from the physical, the spiritual from the material, and the spiritual from the ordinary. Many people see the few minutes spent in a service on Saturday or Sunday as their spiritual time of the week. One big problem: that is not the message of the Bible! And it does not represent a life of holiness. Jesus says to us, our work is a form of worship, and our play is too! The Bible says, "Whatever you do, whether in word or deed, do it to the glory of God." (Colossians 3:17) So, worship happens when we change diapers in the nursery or mow grass or teach a Sunday School class or chaperone a middle school retreat or contribute our tithes and offerings. Jesus calls us to "come and see" and then to "go and tell." The physical and spiritual are intertwined. Our daily bread is more than just food or material possessions. Our daily bread consists of all the resources we have at our disposal.

These few words of the Lord's prayer are significant because we are reminded that our relationship with our Heavenly Father gives us access to His provision. According to Scripture, a father is to provide for his family, not just their physical needs but provide spiritual direction as well. Fathers can get so caught up in the providing for wants that we fail to provide for needs. Scripture is clear: God knows what we need, and He promises to meet all our needs. It started at creation. Look at these Scriptures from Genesis…

> *"I give you every seed-bearing plant*
> *on the face of the whole earth and every tree*
> *that has fruit with seed on it….*
> *I give every green plant for food."*
> **Genesis 1:29-30**

"By the sweat of your brow you will eat your food until you return to the ground since from it you were taken."
Genesis 3:19

"The Lord made garments of skin for Adam and his wife and clothed them."
Genesis 3:21

When Jesus prayed, "Give us today our daily bread," He was reminding us again that we have a right to make requests of our Father. We don't earn that right, it is given to us because of our relationship. Our problem is that we often confuse what we want and what we need. Some people see prayer like a vending machine. They think if you pop in a few words, then out of the slot comes the request, but that's not what prayer is all about.

God's plan was for us to ask, but God doesn't give us everything we ask for. Some people ask for chocolate cake and God gives plain bread because that is what they need. Some people ask for tomorrow's bread and God says:

Wait

Most of us want to skip over the first part of the Lord's Prayer and get to this part of the prayer because this is the asking part, the good stuff, if you will. But we have a Father that provides daily bread and more. A number of years ago, my daughter, Alana, wanted something that I wouldn't give her. Notice I said wanted, not needed. To the best of my knowledge, I have never failed to give her anything she needed, and as I look to the future, I can't imagine a time when I wouldn't give her exactly what she needed if it was within my power. That's part of being a dad. On this occasion, when I failed to respond to her request, she got mad. She told me I was a mean dad, and she wanted a new one. Was I hurt by what she said? No, not really. I understood that she was acting like small children often act. She wanted more than her daily bread. But it made me wonder how often we have gotten mad at God because we wanted more than daily bread. While I was certain I knew what my daughter needed, I'm even more convinced that our Heavenly Father knows exactly what we need, and He has promised to provide it.

God desires to be first in our lives and daily bread has just about everything to do with that priority. If this verse is about resources, then how we go about receiving and saving and disbursing those resources says a lot about how we feel about God. Jesus said in His Sermon on the Mount:

> *"But seek first the kingdom and*
> *His righteousness, and all these things will*
> *be given to you as well."*
> *Matthew 6:33*

"Our daily bread" is included in "all these things." One of my favorite stories from the New Testament is the beach scene after the crucifixion and resurrection of Christ. Simon Peter and some of the boys have been out fishing all night and they had caught nothing. John 21 tells the story if you want to reread it. Jesus is standing on the beach, and he calls out to them, He says FRIENDS, which can also be translated LITTLE CHILDREN, put your nets out on the other side of the boat. They did and caught a net full of fish. While they are making their way to shore, Jesus prepares breakfast for them. Verse 9 says, "when they landed, they saw a fire of burning coals there with fish on it and some bread." Jesus said, "Come and have breakfast." If you remember the story, after breakfast Jesus took Simon Peter for a little walk down the beach. Jesus asked Peter the question: "Do you love me more than these things?" Most Bible scholars believe Jesus was referring to the nets and boat and anchor, and maybe the fish still in the net. You see in one sense, that was Peter's daily bread.

There's nothing wrong with boats and nets and fishing. It was how Peter made his living. And there's nothing wrong with houses and cars and occupations. But Jesus reminds us that the Father and the Kingdom must come first. When He comes first, then we have what we need both spiritually and physically.

Have you discovered yet that dependence is learned in the desert?

When I worked the night shift as a police officer, there was a big bread bakery in the part of town I patrolled. In the early morning hours if you got anywhere near that bakery, you could smell the fresh bread. Sometimes if I had paperwork to do, I would park my patrol car near the bakery and just enjoy the smell. I never saw them bake the bread, but I knew from the smell that there would be fresh bread in the stores.

CALL HOME • LUKE 11:1

I wonder if the Israelites were remembering the smell of freshly baked bread when they found themselves out in the desert. Moses had led them out of slavery in Egypt, but it wasn't long until their stomachs made them grumpy. Listen to what they had to say...

> *"In the desert, the whole community grumbled....you have brought us out into this desert to starve this entire assembly to death."*
> *Exodus 16:2-3*

An empty stomach makes me grumpy too! For forty years the Israelites wandered around the desert, and I'm convinced that most of the reason was because God wanted them to learn dependence. Go back and read Exodus 16 sometime soon and you will see how God provided for them daily. He fed several million of them with something called manna. It was a wafer-like bread that had a honey-like taste. Every morning they got up and went out and collected about half a gallon for each person. It had to be eaten that day, if not, it became infested with worms. There was one exception, and that was the Sabbath. On the day before the Sabbath, they collected enough for two days so they could honor the Sabbath. Miraculously, the manna was good for the second day, but only on the Sabbath.

Do you see the picture? Their bread, or manna, became a symbol of the people's dependence on God. You may be in a desert right now and God is wanting to teach you dependence.

Our need is daily. Perhaps that is why Jesus taught us to pray this simple prayer:

"Give us today..."
Matthew 6:11

Not give us this week or this month or this year. Give us today. Like manna for the children of Israel, we need to ask for it each day, the earlier in your day you ask, the better. Today's supply can't be carried over until tomorrow, and remember, it comes from God.

Though our need is daily, there is a great temptation to take our Supplier for granted. Not long ago, I climbed into my truck and turned the key. All I heard was silence. Now silence is not golden when you turn your key. I popped the hood, got out, and did what I always do when my car has a mechanical problem, I looked under the hood. I have no idea what I'm looking for, but I've seen other people do that, so that's what I did. Although I have limited mechanical knowledge, I did know that my problem might have something to do with the battery. So, I looked at the battery, and the battery looked at me. They have an EYE, you know! I wish they had EARS because I would have had a word or two for the battery. Now the eye I was looking at was green, and green is supposed to be good, but in this case, the eye was just fooling me because the battery was bad.

The battery on a vehicle provides the power to start. Disconnect your battery and you won't go anywhere. Neglect your battery and it won't be long until you won't go anywhere either.

I guess the point I'm trying to make is that you can get by without asking God for your daily bread, but why would you want to try? What would happen if the Lord's Prayer became a part of your daily disciplines? I'm not talking about just saying the words as you brush your teeth or comb your hair, but I'm talking about praying the Lord's Prayer with some intensity and meaning and doing it daily. I think you would see some dramatic improvements in your life. I think you would do more than just get by.

Frustrating to some is the reality that our portions are not even. Have you noticed? Sure you have, but I think it is important to remember that God gives differing amounts of daily bread to each of us, and there is a reason. I think He doesn't give much to some of us because we've proven we can't handle much. In some cases, I think God would love to give us more, but we're not doing anything with what we've got. God promises to supply us with what we need.

One of my memories from childhood is sitting in church on a Sunday night with an older friend. Wayne was a graduate student studying architecture at the University of Houston, and I was about 11 years of age. We attended this small Evangelical Free Church, and I thought a lot of Wayne, so whenever I got the chance, I would sit by him. He never seemed to mind. During this service, the offering plate was passed, and Wayne put in a quarter and kind of laughed. I passed the plate on without contributing. Wayne leaned over to me and said, "I'm a poor college student, what's your excuse?" Wayne understood about as well as anybody I have ever known, that one of the questions God asks is this: What are you going to do with what you've got? I should tell you one other thing about Wayne that I did not learn until several years later. Wayne, the poor college student, paid my way to summer camp. I have no idea where Wayne is today, but I hope he knows he made a good investment with what little he had.

I think daily bread is a lot like the talents in the parable that Jesus told.

> **"To one he gave five talents of money, to another two talents, and to another one talent, each according to his ability."**
> **Matthew 25:15**

If our daily bread can best be described as the resources we need to help us do His will in this world, then we shouldn't count on much unless we have made a commitment to do His will.

You probably haven't given much thought to what it would be like to live in a Third World area where Daily Physical Bread was such a concern, but I came across an exercise – adapted from the U.N. Food and Agriculture Organization's magazine, "Freedom from Hunger," and based on excerpts from The Great Ascent by Robert L. Heilbroner (New York Harper & Row, 1963) – and it may help to get you in touch with the reality of life in the shadows cast by our relative wealth.

First, take out the furniture: leave a few old blankets, a kitchen table, and maybe a wooden chair. You've never had a bed, remember?

Second, throw out your clothes. Each person in the family may keep the oldest suit or dress, a shirt or blouse. The head of the family has the only pair of shoes.

Third, all kitchen appliances have vanished. Keep a box of matches, a small bag of flour, some sugar and salt, a handful of onions, and a dish of dried beans. Rescue those moldy potatoes from the garbage can: those are tonight's meal.

Fourth, dismantle the bathroom, shut off the running water, take out the wiring and the lights and everything that runs by electricity.

Fifth, take away the house and move the family into the tool shed.

Sixth, by now all the other houses in the neighborhood have disappeared; instead, there are shanties – for the fortunate ones.

Seventh, cancel all the newspapers and magazines. Throw out the books. You won't miss them – you are now illiterate. One radio is now left for the whole shantytown.

Eighth, no more postmen, firemen, or government services. The two-classroom school is 3 miles away, but only 2 of your 7 children attend anyway, and they walk.

Ninth, no hospital, no doctor. The nearest clinic is now 10 miles away with a midwife in charge. You get there by bus or bicycle if you're lucky enough to have one.

Tenth, throw out your bankbooks, stock certificates, pension plans, and insurance policies. You now have a cash hoard of $5.

Eleventh, get out and start cultivating your three acres. Try hard to raise $300 in cash crops because your landlord wants one-third and your moneylender 10 percent.

Twelfth, find some way for your children to bring in a little extra money, so you have something to eat most days. But it won't be enough to keep bodies healthy – so lop off 25 to 30 years of life.

Jesus said, "to whom much has been given, much is required." The last time I checked, our portions were pretty big. I guess that means we have a great responsibility. I was reminded of the size of our portions on a trip to Africa. After celebrating at a very rural church in the tiny country of Eswatini (formerly Swaziland), our group from the United States was treated to this amazing lunch that represented so much sacrifice on the part of this small congregation. It was truly humbling because their hospitality far exceeded their resources. As we made our way back to the main road on a primitive path, our vehicle came upon a small group of seven or eight children, siblings, I assumed. It appeared that they were walking to secure water for their family. The children ranged in age from 3 to 13, with the youngest ones riding in a makeshift wheelbarrow and the older ones walking and pushing. Several of the children carried items that could hold water. My friend Doug was driving, but I asked him to stop as I rolled down my backseat window. Reaching into a box of lollipops that Doug carries with him everywhere he goes, I started handing these treats out the window. The smiles were wide, and I was impressed to see the older ones make certain the younger ones got their lollipop first, in case there were not enough to go around. We had plenty and each child received a lollipop. Though the cost of candy was small, the expressions on the faces were priceless. Daily bread, which can mean so little to me because I have plenty, is a desperate need I'm guessing for this little group of children. As we drove away, I was reminded again of how great my portions are and how much responsibility I bear. Help me Lord be a better steward!

Doctors will tell you that you are what you eat. So, lollipops in excess are bad and vegetables and fruits are good. Every week it seems like, there is something new that you shouldn't eat because it is bad for you. And it is always, always something I like! Just once I wish the New England Journal of Medicine would come out with a study that says broccoli or cauliflower is bad for you.

You are what you eat. While that is true Physically, the Bible tells us and I think life confirms that the same is true Spiritually. Way back in the Old Testament these words were spoken.

> **"Man does not live on bread alone,**
> **but on every word that comes**
> **from the mouth of God."**
> ***Deuteronomy 8:3***

Jesus thought those words were so important that He repeated them in Matthew 4:4. In fact, Jesus even told us that He was the Bread of Life. A part of our Daily Bread has to be time spent in God's Word. I know some people try and get enough on Sunday to make it through the week, but it isn't enough because it is through God's Word that God wants to communicate with you daily. If you haven't opened your Bible since last Sunday, then you missed six days of personal messages from Almighty God to You! We are so blessed to have His Word right there to read anytime, day or night. When we feast upon His Word then it changes this prayer dramatically. You see *Give Us Today our Daily Bread* is not a selfish prayer but a prayer where we are volunteering to be empowered and strengthened for service.

Another memory from childhood is sitting down at the breakfast table and seeing a little plastic loaf of bread. Imprinted on the side were the words Our Daily Bread. That little plastic loaf contained Scripture verses to read and embrace with strength for the day. It served as a reminder of the words of Joshua:

> **"Choose you this day who you will serve, but as for me and my house, we will serve the Lord."**
> **Joshua 24:15**

How's your spiritual walk? Is it daily? Are you trying to get by with checking in to church once a week or maybe once a month? Could your life be substantially different if you decided today that you wanted a daily portion of bread? Jesus says simply: All you have to do is Call Home!

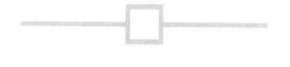

REFLECTION QUESTIONS:

1. Who is the most generous person you have ever known? What do you think made them so giving?

2. What's on your list of daily needs?

3. How has God provided for more than what you need?

4. Do you have more than you need? If so, who might benefit from your excess?

5. Has there been a time in your life when someone surprised you with provision? What's that story?

6. Where might God be calling you to invest with your overflow?

7. Paul told Timothy to "be rich in good deeds." Could you be extravagant with a gift for someone who has a need?

5

When Does the Party Start?

"Forgive us our debts, as we also have forgiven our debtors."

"To forgive is to set a prisoner free and discover that prisoner was you."
Lewis B. Smedes

A one-room schoolhouse shooting near Lancaster, Pennsylvania, captured the attention of people from around the world in October of 2006. Ten young girls were shot, five died, and the gunman took his own life. But perhaps the most remarkable moment in the story came when the family of the perpetrator gathered for the funeral of their son. Upon arrival at the cemetery, they found 40 members of the Amish community directly impacted by this senseless act of violence waiting for them. Their presence was not in protest, they were there to mourn with the family and to offer forgiveness. The power of this act created confusion for many and opened the door for lots of conversation about what it means to choose forgiveness, and I am convinced that it is a choice.

> *"Forgive us our debts, as we also have forgiven our debtors."*

There is no magic in those words. We can say the words, write the words, read the words, and fail to embrace the opportunity afforded to each of us in this portion of the Lord's Prayer. The words have great power, but only when we understand that we, each and every one of us, are in debt spiritually, and we have a need to be forgiven. Many people pray those words but don't see themselves as sinners, debtors, or trespassers. They would never want to admit that they were spiritually bankrupt. In fact, they don't see themselves as guilty before God. Now if you follow that logic, if there is no guilt, then there is no need for forgiveness.

Interestingly enough, there is another large group of people that don't feel completely innocent either. If you are in either one of those categories, the Lord's Prayer then becomes an empty repetition of words.

Now you and I know whether or not we are in debt financially. Businesses are kind enough to send us regular reminders detailing our debt. We understand that there are consequences to not paying our debts. I've never had the experience of receiving a letter from a bank or credit card company or any other kind of business notifying me that my debts had all been forgiven. Such is not the case spiritually. While the Bible confirms that all, every single one of us, have sinned (Romans 3:23 5:12; Psalms 106:6), the primary message of God's Word is the love He has for us and the forgiveness He offers.

When I think about this portion of the Lord's Prayer the word "release" comes to my mind. I chose the word release because I believe that is what happens when we are forgiven. And then we must accept that forgiveness. We tend to remember: _____ (you fill in the blank). And we can choose to carry those things around with us all our lives, and some people do, or we can let them go. We can follow the example of these heartbroken Amish community members, some of who are still dealing with the aftermath of the shooting, and release those memories and their pain to our Father in heaven, whose name is hallowed and who has a plan for your life that only you can live out. He has promised to provide all the resources we need, and there is one thing we all have in common and that is: the need to be forgiven.

As a pastor, I discovered there is a great danger in ministry, especially the preaching ministry, to present an image that is larger than life. It is a humbling experience to stand behind a pulpit and preach the good news. If it doesn't humble you, then you shouldn't be doing it. Hardly a month ever went by that I didn't hear about a fellow pastor that wasn't finishing well. Despite this, people listen to God's messengers, and they hear the stories of God's faithfulness, and soon it sounds like that pastor has never struggled with anything, that he or she never needs to be forgiven. Lest you ever get to thinking that about a pastor, let me assure you all pastors are saved by grace, and forgiveness is something that we need to both receive and to offer daily.

In Jesus' teaching from the Sermon on the Mount, we read that our willingness to forgive is tied directly to our own forgiveness.

> *"For if you forgive other people when they sin against you, your heavenly Father will also forgive you. But if you do not forgive others their sins, your Father will not forgive your sins."*
> *Matthew 6:14-15*

Ouch! These are strong words. No confusion or lack of clarity here. My request for forgiveness is directly connected to my responsibility for offering forgiveness. Jesus didn't have to do that! In fact, there are times when I wish that the two could be treated as completely separate issues. What does my forgiveness have to do with my willingness to forgive? **Jesus says it has everything to do with it.**

Simon Peter is the disciple about whom we know the most. Interestingly enough, lots of what we know about him is based on his failure. Those floundering and failing moments are captured in Scripture for all to read, and I love that the Holy Spirit as editor of the Holy Scriptures did not remove these less-than-stellar moments. It makes the Bible even more real to me.

There is a pattern for forgiveness found in Simon Peter's life that I believe can be helpful for us as we consider how to offer forgiveness and accept forgiveness. By the way, some people, maybe you, are better at extending forgiveness than you are at receiving forgiveness. Join me in looking at three snapshots from the fisherman's life and see how forgiveness was developed. Picture number one comes from what we know as the parable of the unmerciful servant.

Do you remember this story? It starts this way: "Then Peter came up to Jesus and asked, 'Lord, how many times shall I forgive my brother when he sins against me?'" And in typical Peter fashion, he didn't wait for an answer. He answered the question himself: "Up to seven times." Jesus uses Peter's question to teach his disciples a lesson about forgiveness. He tells them the story of a king who went to settle his accounts. One servant owed the king an astronomical amount. It would have taken a daily laborer 150,000 years to repay the king. Because he could not pay his debt, the king ordered the man and his family sold into slavery. But the man fell on his knees and begged for patience and mercy, and he promised to repay the king. At this point the king did a most remarkable thing, he took pity on him, completely canceled the debt, and let him go.

Sounds too good to be true. It is! The spiritual application is easy to see. You and I have a debt that we cannot pay, we could work for the next 150,000 years and the Bible says we couldn't pay it. It is just as impossible for us to pay our spiritual debt as it was for that servant to pay his debt to the king.

Jesus came to earth as our King. He was the bearer of forgiveness. He died on a cross to purchase for us the gift of salvation. In fact, on the cross, do you remember the words

He spoke: "Father, forgive them for they don't know what they are doing." His last words from the cross were: "It is Finished." The Greek word for that is the word: "tetelestai." That word was a commercial word. You've seen the same words stamped across a contract after you have completed your financial obligation. "Tetelestai" means "PAID IN FULL." That is exactly what Jesus did on the cross.

Forgiveness is what makes Christianity unlike any other religion in the world.

There are some tremendously devout people in the world, people that pray multiple times a day. Sometimes they make pilgrimages to far-off places to pray. Often, they fast for long periods of time. Ask them though about forgiveness. They will all tell you the same thing: "We don't know whether or not we are forgiven. We can only hope for the best."

Thankfully, that is not the message of Christ. Listen to these words from 1 John:

"If we claim to be without sin, we deceive ourselves and the truth is not in us. If we confess our sins, He is faithful and just and will purify us from all unrighteousness."
I John 1:8-9

Well, let's go back to the story that Jesus told for just a moment. Remember the servant's debt had been canceled. He then had an obligation to extend the same kind of forgiveness to others. The two are tied together. It is that horizontal and vertical relationship that each of us enjoy. We are connected to God and to each other. One relationship, thriving or suffering, impacts the other. The servant went out after having his debt canceled and found a fellow servant that owed him some money. In this case it was about 100 days worth of work. He grabbed him and began to choke him, demanding payment. His fellow servant fell to his knees and spoke almost the identical words in asking for patience and mercy. But patience and mercy were not extended, and this man was thrown into jail.

An interesting thing happens at this point. Word gets back to the king about what this servant has done. He apparently reinstates the canceled debt and throws the servant into prison reminding him of the mercy that had previously been extended to him. And then there are some words from Jesus that lots of folks would prefer not to read. Jesus says:

> **"This is how my heavenly Father will treat each of you unless you forgive your brother from your heart."**
> **Matthew 18:35**

The message in this parable is simple: find and forgive, be found and forgiven. Receiving forgiveness and extending forgiveness are interdependent but the great news is that forgiveness is available to each of us. Forgiveness is what makes our Christian faith different. God promises to forgive us for all our sins. God's purpose for us is to forgive all those who sin against us. Forgiveness is a gift to be given and received.

Picture number two from the life of Simon Peter takes us to the beach. We explored this earlier, but it's worth visiting again. It's the story of Jesus and Peter in John 21:15-19. It is one of my favorites - Jesus, breakfast, a walk on the beach - add a Labrador retriever and the scene would be perfect. Do you remember the story? Jesus comes and finds Peter. I think that's significant! I'm not sure at that point that Peter wanted to be found after denying Jesus as had been predicted and I'm not sure that if he was going to be found that he would have wanted Jesus to find him where He found him. You see Peter was back doing exactly what he had been doing the first time Jesus found him. He was fishing!

After Jesus cooks breakfast on the beach for the disciples, He and Peter take a walk. On the walk Jesus talked to Peter, not about the past, but about the future. There were no reminders about the denials. Jesus never even raised the subject. He didn't say, "I told you so!" And He could have. He had put it in the past and He was not looking in the rear-view mirror. Never forget:

God remembers what man forgets:
Our Humanness.

Man remembers what God forgets:
Our Sin.

The Psalmist tells us that our sins can be buried deep in the sea of forgetfulness, these sins are separated as far as the east is from the west. I love the story about a preacher's kid who knew his Bible pretty well. He had been out shopping with his mom one day and his behavior had been far from acceptable. On the way home, he was pretty sure he was in trouble. He asked his mom: "When we ask God to forgive us when we are bad, He does, doesn't He?" His mother said, "Yes, He does." The boy continued, "And when He forgives us, He buries our sins in the deepest sea, doesn't He? His mom said, "Yes, that's what the Bible says." The boy was silent for a while and then said, "I've asked God to forgive me, but I bet when we get home, you're going to go fishing for those sins, aren't you?"

That's a temptation for us in our humanity, but not for God. He forgets! The message of the Bible is consistent:

**If you cannot forgive,
then you cannot be forgiven.**

I'm reminded of an article that I cut out of the newspaper many years ago. It came from Fairfax, VA, and it was the story of a father and mother, Louis and Patricia Herzog, who lost their teenage daughter to a drunk driver. They filed a 1.5-million-dollar lawsuit against the 17-year-old that was convicted of drunk driving and manslaughter in the death of their daughter; however, they settled for $936. But here was the catch. The payment had to be made $1 a week for 18 years, the number of years their daughter had lived. According to the article, the parents had been to court four times in eight years to enforce the punishment and they maintained they would continue going to court to make sure that not a week went by without the guilty man being reminded of their daughter's death. The line in the article that caught my eye was the dad's response to the judge's statement that *"to err is human, but to forgive is divine."* He said, "I suppose to forgive is divine, but unfortunately, Lou Herzog is just an average guy."

I agree with Mr. Herzog, to forgive is divine, and you and I are most like God when we forgive. The Hebrew word for forgive is the word "NASA." It is an easy one to remember because it means to "lift away." When we are forgiven, and when we forgive, we are lifting an unnecessary burden out of our life, and that allows us to move forward.

Picture number three from the life of Peter is all about freedom, the freedom that comes from forgiveness and allows us to follow Him. We find Peter, no longer the fisherman but now the preacher. The occasion is his first sermon after the Day of Pentecost. You can read the sermon in Acts 2:14-41.

In this first sermon, Peter preaches a message of repentance. He told the people gathered there that day that everyone who calls on the name of the Lord will be saved. How do we call on the name of the Lord? By praying! "Forgive us our debts, as we forgive our debtors." It doesn't say "when" or "if." Why? Because when you and I come to see ourselves as Debtors in need of someone to cancel our debt, we can't help but forgive those that have sinned against us.

Forgiveness is a choice, but not an option.

You may say that doesn't make sense. How can it be a choice but not an option? You and I must ask for forgiveness, it is our choice. We also must accept forgiveness, another choice. Some people have asked for forgiveness, but they have never accepted forgiveness. But once you have, then you don't have an option about whether you will offer forgiveness. Just as God doesn't allow you to pick who you are going to love, He says, "love everyone, even your enemies," He doesn't allow you to offer selective forgiveness.

> **"Repent and be baptized every one of you, in the name of Jesus Christ for the forgiveness of your sins."**
> **Acts 2:38**

When we don't forget, we collect baggage. It doesn't matter whether it is a little overnight bag or twelve steamer trunks, failing to forgive and forget becomes an obstacle to seeing God's will done in our lives. There are places we cannot go because we have so many bags. There are things God has chosen for us to do, but we can't do them because of the excess weight we are carrying around. The book of Hebrews tells us to throw off everything that hinders us and the sin that so easily entangles us so that we can run the race with perseverance.

There is an old legend about three men and their sacks. Each man had two sacks, one tied in front of his neck and the other tied on his back. When the first man was asked what was in his sacks, he said, "In the sack on my back are all the good things friends and family have done. That way, they're hidden from view. In the front sack are all the bad things that have happened to me. Every now and then, I stop, open the front sack, take the things out, examine them, and think about them." Because he stopped so much to concentrate on all the bad stuff, he really didn't make much progress in life.

The second man was asked about his sacks. He replied, "In the front sack are all the good things I've done. I like to see them, so quite often I take them out to show them off to people. The sack in the back? I keep all my mistakes in there and carry them all the time. Sure, they're heavy. They slow me down, but you know, for some reason, I can't put them down."

When the third man was asked about his sacks, he answered, "The sack in front is great. There I keep all the positive thoughts I have about people, all the blessings I've experienced, and all the great things other people have done for me. The weight isn't a problem. The sack is like the sails of a ship. It keeps me going forward.

"The sack on my back is empty. There's nothing in it. I cut a big hole in its bottom. In there, I put all the bad things that I can think about myself or hear about others. They go in one end and out the other, so I'm not carrying around any extra weight at all."

What are you carrying in your sacks?

What would have happened if Jesus had not found Peter on the beach that day? What could you have expected out of Peter for the rest of his life? I can answer that pretty quickly for you: Not Much! I think you could have found Peter there fishing most days, certainly not being the leader of the early church.

When does the party start? It starts when you are forgiven, and you forgive. With that freedom comes the ability to follow. Peter knew that fishing was great, but it didn't come close to seeing men and women, boys and girls, come to know the Savior and experience the freedom that comes from being forgiven.

One of God's gifts to the Children of Israel was the concept of a year of Jubilee. The 25th chapter of Leviticus tells the story. It worked like this: every fifty years there was to be a great festival of redemption and renewal among the people. During that year, all debts would be forgiven, all servants were released, and everyone was free to return to their original home regardless of the obstacles that might have blocked their way, even if those same obstacles had been in the way for 49 years. Can you imagine how people looked forward to the year of Jubilee? I can hear people now: "you know if I can just hang in there for another 31 years everything is going to be all right!" Or "I can do whatever I want this year because if I can only make it until next year, everything will work out since it is the year of the Jubilee."

We don't live on that side of the cross. We live on this side. There is a huge difference. We don't have to wait for a special year. Our forgiveness and freedom begin the moment we choose it. All we need to do is Call Home!

REFLECTION QUESTIONS:

1. What is more difficult for you, forgiving others or forgiving yourself?

2. Would you have been able to follow the example from the Amish community and attend the funeral service for the individual responsible for this tragedy?

3. What do you imagine was going through Peter's mind as Jesus invited him to take a walk on the beach?

4. Is there someone in your life that needs your forgiveness?

5. Are there other forgiveness stories in Scripture or from your own experience that have encouraged you to accept or offer forgiveness?

6. Do you have a story of offering or accepting forgiveness that might be an encouragement to others?

6

Where Do You Choose to Stand?

"And lead us not into temptation but deliver us from evil (or the evil one)."

"Free cheese is always available in mouse traps."
Unknown

One of the opportunities I have enjoyed for many years is spending lots of time on airplanes. Someone asked me recently how I liked flying so much. I thought about it for a few seconds and realized that it has become so natural for me that I almost don't even think about it. The next day I was on a flight, and it dawned on me that I had failed to hear the flight attendants make the speech about fastening seat belts, oxygen masks falling from the ceiling, and green lights leading to red lights indicating you have reached an exit door. All that started me wondering about how flight attendants make that same speech each time a plane prepares for takeoff, realizing that a large percentage of the people on the plane are paying no attention to them. I confess that I don't listen to them. I did when I first started flying and I paid attention a few years ago when I was on a very large plane that had three sections. The flight was not very full, so I asked if I could sit in the back section to get some work done. It turned out that no one else sat back there, so I felt obligated to listen when the flight attendant gave her demonstration of seat belts and oxygen masks.

Why don't we listen? While I'm guessing there are a host of reasons, I'm wondering if it is because we only need the information in case of an emergency and most of us don't want to think about being involved in an emergency on a plane. I've spent lots of hours on airplanes, and it occurred to me that maybe we treat the words of the Lord's Prayer a little like some of us treat the words uttered by flight attendants during their pre-flight routine. The words of the Lord's Prayer for many of us are so familiar that we say them or hear them and never really pray them unless we encounter an emergency. This portion of the Lord's Prayer addresses the alarm bells of an emergency. Jesus prayed, "lead us not into temptation, but deliver us from evil."

Temptation…someone once said this:

"Opportunity knocks once, temptation knocks the door down."

CALL HOME • LUKE 11:1

What have you never been tempted to do? While that is a personal question, I took a little survey of some friends and loved their responses. Here is a random sampling of answers to the statement, "I've never been tempted to…" and you can add your thoughts to the list.

- eat Oreos without milk!
- enter any kind of eating contest.
- give advice.
- go parachuting, learn to fly, bungee jump, rock climb, ride in an F 15 or generally anything that requires me to fly, jump, or free fall.
- eat sushi while skydiving naked. (one of my more unusual friends!)
- under no circumstances would I be tempted to sleep on the side of a mountain, let alone climb a mountain.
- steal just one piece of candy from those "help yourself" bins at the grocery store.
- go streaking!

Finally, my personal favorite…

- answer questions about anything for fear that it might end up in a sermon or worse yet, a book!

As I was driving, I was reminded of some things I've never been tempted to do. I saw a big sign advertising in huge letters: Body Piercing: Ears, Nose, Navel – I've never been tempted to have my body pierced. A short distance from that sign I saw some men painting on one of those big water towers while hanging off the side. I also watched a guy de-icing a plane this week in 4-degree temperatures. Never had the slightest temptation. I've also never been tempted to order broccoli in a restaurant.

You can see that our lack of temptation has lots to do with food, high places, and pain. Now most of us feel comfortable sharing those things that we have never been tempted to do, but what if I turned the question around this morning and asked you the question:

What tempts you the most?

And maybe if I got more specific and asked you the question: What tempts you the most and you know God disapproves? I think those answers might go unspoken. Those aren't things we like to think about, much less talk about.

The poet, James Dickey, wrote a book called *Deliverance, Deliverance*. You might be more familiar with the movie that used only half the title. It is the story of four city men, suburbanites, who take a canoe trip down a wild white-water river in North Georgia. On the way, two of them are ambushed and one is raped by murderous locals. They make a hair-raising escape, and the rest of the story is about their hazardous trip down the canyon, with one of the locals stalking and shooting at them from above. When they finally reach safety, they cannot even talk about their ordeal. They are delivered…barely…but their minds are scarred for life. What

James Dickey really wrote was a modern morality play. Life itself is like the passage down a wild primitive canyon, where we are easy marks because temptation is all along the way. Like these men when they began their outing, we often manage to laugh and sing and pretend we are having fun. But the evil and evil one is always there, lying in wait, ready to spring out and devour us.

It is in this kind of life that Jesus gave us a Model Prayer: The Lord's Prayer. And perhaps the strangest line of the prayer is:

"Lead us not into temptation…."

Why would God want to do that? Maybe the better questions are:

Do we really understand the part that temptation plays in the Christian life? And do we understand the role that Satan plays in this life?

When Jesus taught about temptation, He had already been through temptation. He had first-hand experience. Matthew 4 and Luke 4 tell us the story. Study the three temptations of Jesus and you will discover that all three had one thing in common: they were all appeals to let self, and not God, stand at the center of the universe. The real question regarding temptation is:

Where do you choose to stand?

The Lord's Prayer is a prayer, I believe, for people who have chosen to commit their lives to Christ. Throughout the

Bible, we read the stories of God's people who have been tempted and the question being asked each time: Where do you choose to stand? It was asked of Abraham and Sarah as they waited and waited for the promise of a child. There was Joseph who found himself in both a pit and a prison. How about Moses, who for forty years was tending sheep on the backside of nowhere? There was Daniel, one of Israel's best and brightest, taken captive. In the New Testament we read about Simon Peter who in a critical hour denied Christ. The Apostle Paul was imprisoned because of his faith.

Every time there was the opportunity for the tempter, Satan, to celebrate. But every time the celebration was short-lived. God ended up using those pits and prisons and deserts and dungeons to do something good. May we never forget that Satan has no power except the power that God permits.

I love the promise found in 1 John 4:4:

"God's Spirit who is in you, is greater than the devil who is in the world."

Temptation can be used to do some great work in our lives if we resist, overcome, and in some cases, flee from temptation. There is a refining process God can use as He develops the character of those who choose faithfulness.

Webster defines temptation as: *to entice to do wrong by the promise of pleasure or gain.* Temptation is simply an appeal to self. And temptation is natural! As long as evil is allowed to exist in this world, we will always be presented with the opportunity to do wrong. Don't be surprised! If I asked: How many have ever been tempted? The response would be 100%. Every single person is familiar with temptation. Temptation is a choice, no more, no less. It is not sin. It isn't good or bad, simply an alternative to God's will. The choice always involves the use of the legitimate in an illegitimate way. Perhaps the most controversial thought about temptation is that it is necessary. Really? I believe it is. We learn a lot about ourselves in how we respond to temptation. Temptation allows us opportunities for obedience. It can build a holy character and reform our lives to gain God's best. Our time here on earth is a time of preparation. Temptation is a part of that preparation. The Apostle Paul had an impressive resume. Few could deny that. I'm not sure why - Scripture indicates that maybe it was to keep him humble - but Paul dealt with a continual problem in his life. Notice Paul's testimony about temptation he faced and how it refined his character:

> *"To keep me from becoming conceited because of these surpassingly great revelations, there was given me a thorn in my flesh, a messenger of Satan, to torment me."*
> *2 Cor. 12:7*

While we can only speculate Paul's persistent problem, we know that Paul prayed to have that thorn removed and as far as we know it never was. There was a purpose. Notice the messenger was from Satan. We don't know whether the messenger was a pain, a problem, or a person who was a pain and maybe a problem. What we do know from verse 8 in that same chapter is that Paul pleaded with God three times to take it away. Do you remember God's Response?

> ***"My grace is sufficient for you; my power is
> made perfect in weakness."***
> ***2 Corinthians 12:9***

The Apostle Paul, like Job, and the first-century church in Smyrna, and a host of others, that includes you and me, are in a refining process. One of my favorite verses is Job 23:10:

> ***"But he knows the way that I take, when He
> has tested me, I will come forth as gold."***

Job offers a testimony of man not on the other side of the refiner's fire, but in the heart of it. And that is so powerful!

One of my jobs when our kids were at home was to wake them up and prepare them for school. Some days this is easier said than done. I've discovered that it took different strategies to get them up and out of bed. With our son, Andy, I could leave the light off and just pat him on the arm and talk to him. Pretty soon, he is conversing and then he is up and going. Our daughter, Alana, was a whole different story! Because her little motor ran so hard during the day, she slept just as hard at night. I had a completely different strategy with her. I would go in and turn on radios and lights, tickle her ears, pat her on the back, the whole nine yards. Finally, I had to resort to picking her up out of the bed and making her walk to wake her up.

That's kind of a simple illustration, but I think it describes the strategies that God employs with some of us. There are some of us that just need a little tap on the shoulder. We may sense God's communicating to us through a sermon or a song. The very nature of our personality may be that we want to do what pleases God most of the time. But on the other hand, some of us need a two-by-four upside the head on a regular basis. We just don't seem to get it. Adam and Eve were the first to fall, but they weren't the last. Their experience offers us an excellent look at the process of temptation. It hasn't changed in all these years.

I'm not certain where I found this strategy but somewhere along the way I discovered six steps on the road of temptation that leads to sin based on the experience of Adam and Eve. See if you can identify with this dangerous process:

1. We are given the false impression that whatever we do wrong is not that serious.

"You will certainly not die, the serpent said to the woman." Genesis 3:4

The devil leads Adam and Eve to believe that eating the forbidden fruit would not really have any serious consequences. Have you ever rationalized away temptation believing that it wasn't really that big a deal?

2. We see, in fact or in our minds, something or someone or some situation that appeals to our selfishness.

> ***"For God knows that when you eat from it your eyes will be opened, and you will be like God, knowing good from evil."***
> ***Genesis 3:5***

Satan presented the picture of Adam and Eve becoming as gods, knowing good and evil, if they ate the forbidden fruit. While you may not have pictured yourself as a god, I'm guessing that selfishness has been at the root of your sin, it certainly has been true for me.

3. A powerful response is produced within us.

> ***"When the woman saw that the fruit of the tree was good for food and pleasing to the eye, and also desirable for gaining wisdom she took some and ate it. She also gave some to her husband, who was with her and he ate it."***
> ***Genesis 3:6***

There was great appeal! Temptation holds great appeal, it arouses desires to become great and wise. Tastes good, looks good, makes you wise, how can you possibly resist!

4. We toy with the idea. We entertain it. We play with it. We give ground. The appeal increases. Read verse 6 again and it is easy to see the progression from curious to hooked.

5. We act on what was presented.

> *"Then the eyes of both of them were opened, and they realized that they were naked; so they sewed fig leaves together and made coverings for themselves."*
> **Genesis 3:7**

They reached out and took the fruit. They accepted it. They ate it. This was SELF-WILL against GOD'S WILL. This is the transition from temptation to sin. Finally,

6. We hide the defeat.

> *"Then the man and his wife heard the sound of the Lord God as He was walking in the garden in the cool of the day, and they hid from the Lord in the cool of the garden."*
> **Genesis 3:8**

We try and hide. Our church attendance becomes lax and our Bible remains unopened. Days pass without praying. We are attempting to hide. Exactly what Adam and Eve did. With defeat comes depression as our open communication with God is damaged.

Here are three examples from Scripture of God's attempt to reach the hard-hearted and they all involve Satan serving as God's servant.

> "The next day an <u>evil spirit from God</u>
> came forcefully upon Saul."
> 1 Samuel 18:10

> "<u>Hand this man over to Satan</u>,
> so that the sinful nature may be destroyed,
> and his spirit saved on the day of the Lord."
> 1 Corinthians 5:5

> "Some have rejected these and so
> have shipwrecked their faith. Among
> them are Hymenaeus and Alexander,
> whom I have <u>handed over to Satan</u> to be
> taught not to blaspheme."
> 1 Timothy 2:19-20

The principle is this: **There are times when hearts grow so hard and ears so dull that God turns us over to endure the consequences of our choices.** Why? Maybe so that like the prodigal son, we will come to our senses and be drawn back to the arms of a God that loves us. Sound drastic? It is! It is Tough Love. A love that lets people experience their own hell on earth in hopes that maybe they won't spend eternity in hell.

They tell me that the higher up you go in football, the more time you spend indoors. When Andy was playing football in Middle School, I was recruited to videotape the games. The coaches used the videotapes to teach the players where they were making mistakes, but probably 90% of their time was spent on the football field. Once he got to high school, their time watching film increased as they scouted their opponents, but still most of their time was spent outdoors. Colleges spend more time indoors and finally when you get to the professional level, you spend more time inside studying film than you do outdoors. Professional coaches will watch film over and over and over again. You know what they are looking for: tendencies and weaknesses. And when they find one, they've got their opponent.

The Bible says that we have an enemy, the devil, who prowls around looking for someone to devour. And he studies our game film. He knows our weaknesses. He knows our tendencies. Satan's major enemy is the church. God tells us that temptation can renew the church when we face it down and we are victorious, but we have to understand that:

Life is a test that leads to a choice.

But it's my favorite kind of test: OPEN BOOK. We have the answers. In the Bible we are told of lots of ways of winning. We can be delivered because the Bible promises us that God is always there, with us every single step on the path. Another way we can be delivered is through the common sense that God has endowed us with in order to avoid temptation. We can make great decisions and avoid places (and maybe people) and keep off the path of many dangerous obstacles. And, if all else fails, God has given us the ability to battle temptation.

Notice these verses…

> "Simon, Simon, Satan has asked to sift
> you as wheat. But I have prayed for you,
> Simon, that your faith may not fail.
> And when you have turned back,
> <u>strengthen your brothers</u>."
> Luke 22:31-32

> "No temptation has seized you except
> what is common to man. And God is faithful;
> He will not let you be tempted beyond
> what you can bear. But when you are
> tempted, He will also provide a way out so
> that you can stand up under it."
> 1 Corinthians 10:13

The Nobel Prize winning Swedish author, Lagerkvist, was an agnostic, but ironically, he had a vision for what many Christians have never seen. Many years ago, he wrote the novel, *Barabbas*. There is a scene in the novel that is especially powerful. Barabbas was the criminal that was released instead of Jesus and in the novel, he becomes a Roman slave and is transported to Cyprus where he works in the copper mines. There he meets an old Armenian slave named Sahak, who is a devout follower of Christ. Each slave wears a metal disk proclaiming that he belongs to Caesar. But Sahak has strange markings on the back of his disk which spells out the name Christos Jesus. Although he belongs to Caesar, his real allegiance is to Christ. Professing that he too wishes to follow the Galilean, Barabbas asks that his disk be inscribed with the name of Jesus. Working secretly down in the copper mine, they scratch upon it the same markings that are on Sahak's. But someone overhears and they are reported to the supervisor, who tells the governor of the island. Sahak and Barabbas are brought before him. He questions them about the markings and Sahak says they are the name of his god. The governor reminds him that Caesar is a god also and warns him that having other gods before Caesar is punishable by death. The governor questions Barabbas. Does he believe in this god whose name is inscribed on his disk? Barabbas shakes his head. "You don't?" ask the governor. "Why do you bear his name on your disk then?" Barabbas is silent. "Is he not your god?" asks the governor. "Isn't that what the inscription means?" "I have no God." Barabbas answers at last, so softly that his words are barely audible. Sahak gives him a look of such despair and pain and amazement that it seems to pass right through him, into his inner self, even though he keeps his eyes averted. Once more Sahak is questioned. Does he realize the consequences of wearing the name of his god? YES. "If you renounce your faith no harm shall come to you," says the governor. "Will you do it?" "I cannot," says Sahak. The governor orders him to be taken away and crucified. "Extraordinary man," he says as he looks after him. Then he takes a knife and holding Barabbas' disk in one hand, crosses out the name of Jesus. "There's really no need," he says, "as you don't believe in him in any case." And he commends Barabbas for being a sensible fellow, and orders that he be given a better job. For the rest of his life, Barabbas wears the crossed-out name of Jesus.

Barabbas had chosen where to stand!
Could it be that is what this part of the prayer is all about?

> **"Lead us not into temptation but
> deliver us from evil."**

Where will you stand? Will you keep standing even when it is not the most popular thing to do? Will you endure hardship and maybe even persecution? Will you proudly bear the name: Christian?

There is a great Scripture that many people quote as a verse guaranteeing you can never fall. That's not my interpretation, but I certainly respect those who have that interpretation. But to me, it is a verse about who you can turn to and the power that is available to keep you from falling, but it is still a choice.

> **"To Him who is able to keep you from
> falling and to present you before His glorious
> throne without fault and with great joy—
> to the only God our Savior be glory, majesty,
> power and authority, through Jesus
> Christ our Lord, before all ages,
> now and forevermore."**
> **Jude 24**

Many years ago, I got up at 3:30 a.m. to catch a 6:30 a.m. flight from Kansas City to Houston. The roads were icy, and it was snowing and sleeting all the way to the airport. Runways had to be cleared and so our flight was delayed. We finally boarded the plane at 7:30 a.m. For the next five hours we sat on the plane and on the ground. The place was de-iced seven times! Finally, our plane took off at 12:30 p.m. with the wind howling and the snow falling. At the time I was living in San Diego where we never had weather like I had experienced in those five hours. But here's the amazing thing, ten minutes into that flight to Houston we had climbed through the clouds, left the snow and sleet behind and up above the clouds it was crystal clear blue skies with the sun shining! I'd seen it before, and I've seen it since, and it never ceases to amaze me.

I think that is exactly what happens when we call home, when we really pray. I don't mean simply reciting a memorized prayer, I mean getting on our knees and humbling ourselves before God as we offer our praise, and we present our requests. When we follow the example of Jesus and we spend time in prayer, no matter how dark the clouds are, no matter how many trials and temptations, pains, and problems we are dealing with, if we keep on praying, we finally break through the clouds and the sun is still shining, and we are delivered from evil. It happens when we simply call home!

REFLECTION QUESTIONS:

1. Just for fun, name three things that you have never been tempted to do.

2. Can you identify with the process Adam and Eve experienced when they were tempted in the garden? What's been your best antidote to temptation?

3. What Scripture verse or story have you found most helpful in responding to temptation?

4. What advice would you give to a young Christian about avoiding and overcoming temptation?

5. Have you watched someone deal effectively with temptation and what have you observed?

6. Power, popularity, and pride are three common temptations, what is at the root of each of them and how would you counsel someone who was dealing with one of these temptations?

7. Has there been a time when you battled with temptation and were successful and is there a lesson you learned that could be shared?

7

Who Gets the Last Word?

"For yours is the kingdom, and the power, and the glory forever. Amen"

"Mortals have elaborate plans, but God has the last word."
Eugene Peterson

I've never been very good at benedictions. The benediction is traditionally the last word. I think I've always been more worried about getting in the first word. I know people that seem to have just the right words to conclude. Their words just flow off their tongues or off their pens. I always struggle with the last line of a letter. I know how important that final thought is and so I may sit and look at the computer for what seems like hours trying to come up with that last sentence.

As we come to the end of this magnificent prayer we call the Lord's Prayer, it provides a spectacular benediction.

> *"For yours is the Kingdom, the Power,*
> *and the Glory, forever. Amen."*
> **(NIV)**

> *"You're in charge! You can do anything you want! You're ablaze in beauty! Yes! Yes! Yes!"*
> **(The Message)**

The amen or the benediction to the prayer is something that is only printed in about half of the translations. The New International Version lists it as a footnote. It is a simple, yet powerful way to end such a beautiful prayer. In the previous chapters we have looked at a model Jesus gave that we could use as we approach God with boldness. Simply put, God wants us to call home. He wants to have an ongoing, how's it going, I need help, listen closely kind of continuing conversation with each of us.

I wonder if God feels like I sometimes felt in trying to talk with my kids about their day at school. Whenever I was traveling, I called home at least once every day and when I would ask my teenage son about his day, I almost always got the same response: "Just a regular day." I will never forget asking my daughter about her day in second grade as she too had a normal response: "I can't tell you." The truth is, some days, I'm not sure I wanted to know what she did.

God knows what we do, what we say, and what we think and yet He still wants us to talk to Him. I think there is great significance there. We are given a wonderful reminder in these final words of the Lord's Prayer:

> "For yours is the **kingdom**, the **power**,
> and the **glory**, forever."

The words serve as a message about who is ultimately in charge and who has the final word about everything. Notice the most important word in this benediction. Do you see it?

The key word is **YOURS**, not **MINE**.

On more than one occasion in my life, I've found myself in situations where I have seen first-hand the sickness of our society. The sickness is not cancer or heart disease or any other catastrophic illness. The disease is the virus of self. We live in a world and a culture that glorifies self. Don't believe me, check out social media posts.

One of the great gifts God gave us was the power to choose and the choice comes down to God's way or my way every time. It is an issue of control. Who is going to be in charge? Who makes the final decision? Many people revel in the message of Frank Sinatra's famous song: "I Did it My Way!" I confess that at times, I feel like the selfishness of the world is winning. God knew about our self-centered culture and He inspired people like the Apostle Paul to write these words:

> *"God raised Him from the dead*
> *and set Him on a throne in deep heaven,*
> *in charge of running the universe,*
> *everything from galaxies to governments,*
> *no name and no power is exempt from His*
> *rule. And not just for the time being but*
> *forever. He is in charge of it all, has the*
> *final word on everything."*
> **Ephesians 1:22-23 (The Message)**

Don't miss that last line: He oversees it all, He has the final word on everything. Don't think for a minute that we are the boss! We are only stewards. We may have a word, but we don't have a final word. We acknowledge that fact when we pray these words:

> **"For yours is the Kingdom, and the Power,**
> **and the Glory, forever. Amen."**

We are reminding ourselves, not God, about who gets the last word. The benediction in this prayer teaches us how to finish well. When we pray, "yours is the kingdom," we acknowledge that God has the right to answer prayer in His way. Remember, it's His Kingdom, not ours! Kingdoms have kings and when we pray this benediction, we are recognizing God as the King of our life. We acknowledge that He knows what is best for the Kingdom and that means, He knows what is best for us.

Lots of folks try to build little kingdoms. It may be a business or a hobby. It can be a school, a family, or even a church.

CALL HOME • LUKE 11:1

And they get so wrapped up in what is happening in their little kingdom that they lose their perspective. Here are a couple of verses that remind me that I need God's perspective, moment by moment.

> *"Don't shuffle along, eyes to the ground,*
> *absorbed with the things right in front of you.*
> *Look up and be alert to the things going on*
> *around Christ—that's where the action is.*
> *See things from His perspective."*
> *Colossians 3:1-2 (The Message)*

It is an absolute battle to maintain the proper perspective. We can start thinking that we are the king and we have a kingdom. And I confess I have probably seen this happen more in the church than anywhere else. When it is our kingdom, then we expect things to be done our way. But God is good to give us lots of reminders that the kingdom doesn't belong to us.

A couple of years ago, our family vacationed in a part of Colorado that features the Collegiate Peaks. Named after Harvard, Princeton, and Yale, these mountains are a challenge for those that are inclined to climb them. The kingdom, the power, and the glory are three mountains that we are often tempted to climb. In the previous chapter we looked at temptation and the kingdom and the power and the glory are three powerful attractions.

God is majestic. Jesus is the Messiah. We are neither. Majesty was not reserved for us. We are children of the King and joint heirs with Jesus, but may we never forget our role as servants in the Kingdom. Our responsibility is to help the world, not save it. When I gain the proper perspective, then I am capable of the right response and that is faith, now faith, mustard seed (or bigger) faith to believe that God answers our prayers.

That's what God wants from us. Faith to believe He answers our prayers and complete trust with timing and decisions in answers to our prayers. Kings don't have to consult with a Cabinet or a Congress or their Subjects. Kings are Sovereign. The Lord's Prayer gives us multiple opportunities to petition our King on our behalf, but ultimately, if we end the right way, we leave the answers in His hands. There is tremendous freedom in not being the King. When I get in trouble, and I'm guessing when you get in trouble, is when we forget that it is not our Kingdom but His.

How about power? Do you believe God has the ability to give you what you ask? I believe it is a question of how big is your God? Your vision of God may have lots to do with the men in your life. If you have been let down or left out or maybe even mistreated or abused by the men in your life, then I wouldn't be at all surprised if your vision of God is way too feeble. Some of the healthiest people I know are men and women that had a father that became a miniature picture of what their Heavenly Father was all about. Not all of us were blessed that way, so we need some reminders about God's power. Have you ever watched the fury of a storm? When I lived in San Diego, we seldom had storms, but I remember several of us having lunch near the Pacific Ocean one day because the waves were up, and I wanted to see it. There is something about storms that remind me of the power of God's creation.

That's power in a negative sense. But I'm reminded of the storm that threatened to capsize the disciples' boat one night. When they looked for Jesus, they found Him asleep. They wanted Him to help bail water. Instead, He spoke words.

Can I remind you that is all that needs to happen for God to act and answer prayer?

He simply has to speak the word. He has that kind of power. The Psalmist recognized it. He testified…

"With God we will gain the victory…"
Psalm 60:12

Some years ago, a sociologist accompanied a group of mountain climbers on an expedition. He made lots of observations but one of his most significant was the relationship between cloud cover and contentment. When there was no cloud cover and the peak was in plain view, the climbers were energetic and cooperative. But when the gray clouds covered the view of the mountaintop, the climbers became sullen and selfish.

Like those climbers, I'm convinced that we need to see God's power. We need to hear the stories of God's faithfulness in the lives of our loved ones and friends. We need to share the joys and sorrows of our journey. Why? Because without them we are tempted to climb the mount of self-sufficiency.

God created us remarkably self-sufficient and some of us stubbornly independent. With very little encouragement we can begin to believe that we are powerful. Instead of bowing our knees, we just roll up our sleeves and work a little harder, put in a little longer day. That may help us build a business or make a living, but I promise you it won't make a life! I saw a sign once that said, "The problem with a self-made man is that he worships his creator." It's true! So, what is the proper response? Anchor yourself in hope believing that your future is bright because God is in control.

Lots of verses remind us of this promise, but here is a favorite of many:

> *"For I know the plans I have for you,*
> *plans to give you a hope and a future…."*
> *Jeremiah 29:11*

What a wonderful message from God's Word that is available to each of us when we seek Him with all our heart. Turn off your power long enough to listen to your heart. God has plans for you, He has a future for you. There is hope. When we pray, we are seeking Him, we are pinning our hopes on Him.

Kingdom, power, and finally, glory. Who gets the credit for all your blessings? The key word there is ALL. When we pray, *"Yours is the Glory,"* we are thanking God even before we hear an answer to our prayers. God doesn't need us to give Him credit. He doesn't need us to praise Him. Jesus said, *"if we don't the rocks will cry out."* Giving Him glory is the natural response of someone who hallows His name. There will come a day when every knee bows and every tongue confesses that Jesus Christ is Lord, but praying this portion of the Lord's prayer means we are not waiting for that day. We are getting a head start on heaven.

Depending on the kind of church you grew up in, you may or may not have heard people say: "Amen" or "Praise the Lord." Noisy churches use those words often and with boldness. Those are words that traditionally have been ways of giving God the credit for all your blessings. They are words that when said with sincere hearts bring God glory.

If you grew up in a quiet church, those words might seem rather strange to you. I not only heard those words in services growing up, but we also sang a great little song where the chorus was simply the word: "Amen." It is an exclamation point on God's kingdom, power, and glory.

Can I remind you amen is not a new word? It goes all the way back to the Old Testament. The first record we have of the word amen was a liturgical response in the Book of Numbers. It is part of a ritual for cursing a woman who had been condemned for adultery. After the priest pronounced the curse, the woman herself was to reply amen, amen. (Numbers 5:22) Later on in Deuteronomy, Moses instructs the people to say amen after a curse for anyone who makes a graven or molten image. In the Hebrew language the word amen means: SO, BE IT!

Sometime after its initial use, amen came to be a corporate response in ratifying a covenant with God. We see that in 2 Chronicles.

> *"For great is the Lord and most worthy of praise.... Praise be to the Lord, the God of Israel, from everlasting to everlasting. Then all the people said, 'Amen' and 'Praise the Lord.'"*
> *1 Chronicles 16:25, 36*

So, the next time you hear someone say amen or praise the Lord, or even better, the next time you are tempted to say amen or praise the Lord, don't resist that temptation. Say It! That is a way you can give God glory and it might keep you from pursuing applause.

Of the three temptations: majesty, self-sufficiency, and now applause, this is the one that has the most appeal. We like it when people applaud our efforts, our talent, and our ability. Only one problem, it isn't ours. It is His! He is the owner; we are the managers. And our proper response is to submit ourselves to God completely in love.

When we pray this benediction, and we say "amen," we are doing just that - offering ourselves to Him completely. Amen is one of the most expressive and powerful exclamations in the world. You may not know this, but it is the same word in every language. You could go to a cathedral in Paris, a grass hut in the jungles of Africa, or a concrete block church in Mexico and you could listen to the Lord's Prayer and be assured of knowing at least one word. Amen is the same in every language.

After the death and resurrection of Jesus, who gave us the Lord's Prayer as a model for all our praying, the early Christians always uttered the amen through Jesus Himself.

CALL HOME • LUKE 11:1

Jesus became the guarantor of the prayer. The Apostle Paul expressed this to the Corinthians.

> *"Whatever God has promised gets stamped with the Yes of Jesus. In Him, this is what we preach and pray, the great Amen, God's Yes and our Yes together, gloriously evident. God affirms us, making us a sure thing in Christ, putting His Yes within us."*
> **2 Corinthians 1:17-20 (The Message)**

Do you know what a guarantor is? It is one that stands behind the promise. If you are the guarantor on a promissory note, then you are providing the guarantee that the note will be paid. What a beautiful picture!

When was the last time you called home? I love, love, love when my children and grandchildren call me. If for some reason I miss their call, I will call them back, every single time. It is guaranteed...they are my kids!

When we call our heavenly home through prayer, we never get a voice mail, we never get a busy signal, we never get put on hold, and we never have to worry about being hung up on. Our Father is anxious to talk with us, even if it has been, or maybe especially if, it has been just a regular day. Call home...right now!

REFLECTION QUESTIONS:

1. Would you rather have the first word or the last word in a conversation and why?

2. What are some of the obstacles or challenges for you in prayer?

3. What spiritual discipline or practice helps you get God's perspective?

4. Of the three attractions: majesty, self-sufficiency, or applause, which one are you most often tempted to pursue?

5. What word or phrase would best describe your faith capacity right now? (Mustard seed – mountain moving – something in between)

6. How do you feel when someone close to you calls you and only wants to do all the talking?

7. Write a benediction that best describes what is going on in your life at the moment?

8

What's Next?
Conclusion

"Prayer does not fit us for the greater work:
prayer is the greater work."
Oswald Chambers

Are you a person that prays or a praying person? There is a difference, I believe. And I'm still learning what it means to be that praying person who intercedes for others, asks God for miracles, and waits in silence to hear His voice. Writing a book about prayer has been a part of the journey for me, but I have so much more to learn, and I'm guessing you do too.

Sitting at breakfast with a friend several months ago he offered a bit of a confession to me. He told me that as a pastor, he had become convinced that he was a pastor that prayed, but he had failed to be a praying pastor. As I pondered his confession, I could identify. While prayer has been a part of my life since my earliest memories, I could identify as a pastor and now a president who prays, but I didn't see myself as a praying president.

Pastors get called on often to pray and I've discovered that it happens often to university presidents as well. But offering prayers whether at New Student Orientations, Homecomings, Commencements, or Dedications doesn't qualify me as a Praying President. I'm still in the president that prays category if my prayers are limited to events, meetings or even my early morning quiet time.

So here is my confession to you: **I want to be a praying person**.

What's next for each of us as we call home and talk to our Heavenly Father? How can prayer be more than a routine or a regular habit in our lives? Where does God want to take us in this ongoing conversation about all the details and decisions we face each day? After all, Scripture tells us that He knows the very number of hairs on our heads and His eye is on the sparrow!

Let me suggest that in order to have this continuing conversation with God it makes sense to start your day with Him. While it is true that we can pray any time and all the time, when we fail to begin our day in prayer it is a bit like the football player that skips the locker room and enters the field of play without the proper equipment. Every day has "enough trouble of its own," and beginning and ending our day with a divine appointment makes too much sense to be skipped.

Zig Ziglar suggested that love is spelled T I M E, and I believe he was right. One of the ways we demonstrate our love for God is by making time with God the priority in our life. Starting the day with prayer and finishing the day with prayer makes this ongoing conversation so much more possible and powerful. The Lord's Prayer provides a wonderful opening prayer to the day, and I love setting the stage for nighttime dreams by offering these same words to Jesus. My days get filled up with appointments, important meetings, and the privilege of spending time with special people, but all that pales in comparison to the significance of resting in God's presence and hearing the Spirit's voice speak truth into my life. But without establishing those regular prayer times to commune with the Father, my life can get off track quickly and I can become so busy believing I am making a difference that I miss the message and the moments God has preordained for me in calling home.

The dramatic impact of this time is illustrated time and time again in the life of Jesus. In Mark's Gospel, the very first chapter, we read these words as paraphrased by Eugene Peterson:

> ***While it was still night, way before dawn,***
> ***he got up and went out to a secluded spot***
> ***and prayed. Simon and those with him***
> ***went looking for him. They found him***
> ***and said, "Everybody's looking for you."***
> ***Mark 1:35-37***

If I asked you to tell me about your all-time, very busiest day, it could not match what Jesus experienced leading up to this moment way before dawn when he goes to a secluded spot to pray.

From time to time my wife or kids will ask me about my day and on more days that I would like to admit I find myself thinking, "I can't even begin to describe to you the kinds of meetings I was in or the decisions I had to make today!"

Jesus' day here in Mark 1 was one of teaching, exorcisms, an invitation to dinner that prompted a need for healing, and then at the end of the day, here is the way it is described:

> ***That evening, after the sun was down,***
> ***they brought sick and evil-afflicted***
> ***people to him, the whole city lined***
> ***up at his door! He cured their sick***
> ***bodies and tormented spirits.***
> ***Mark 1:32-33 (The Message)***

Have you ever had the whole city, or campus, or church or family lined up at your door or at least it felt like it? And what did Jesus do? He determined that in this crazy "everybody wants/needs something time," it would be best to get up in the middle of the night, way before dawn, find a solitary place and pray.

> ***Scripture reveals not a Jesus that***
> ***prayed but a praying Jesus.***

Now I know there might be one or two reading the book who are prone to cynicism, so let me try and read your mind for a moment: "Person that prays or a praying person…isn't that just an arrangement of words?" And you would be right, but I'm convinced, at least in my own life, that there is a difference and I want to be a person who prays, calling home at all hours of the day and night.

How about a place? Do you have a solitary place or at least a special place where you can be alone to call home? Any place or space is made holy when we invite Jesus to join us. Over the years I've known of people who had prayer closets, basement corners, and even unoccupied cubicles where they spent their quiet time in prayer. In my own life, I have always tried to find a place free of as many distractions as possible. My mind is prone to wander, and I can be easily diverted, and it happens in a flash. These days I love time in a chair with an ottoman in the corner of our bedroom. The chair provides a great place to read Scripture and the ottoman serves as a comfortable altar. The richness and refreshment that comes from praying and remembering moments in the past where God has spoken to me in this spot are rich. In my office at the university, I love kneeling on a rug knitted by a young woman in Africa who found a safe place to recover and heal. Purchasing the rug from her as a special place to call home has blessed me far more than the money she received from me for her beautiful handiwork. When I travel I look for new places so that I won't miss my appointments with God. Find a time. Find a place. Make time. Make space. God has a message for each of us, and it is tailored for this time in our life. Don't you dare miss it! Challenges come our way when we get too busy and skip our appointments with our Father who is waiting on us to call.

In chapter 11 of *A Burning in my Bones*, Winn Collier shares a story of a board meeting at Christ Our King Church where Eugene Peterson was the pastor. Peterson goes to the church board meeting that night after a tough conversation with his 5-year-old daughter, Karen, who had asked him to read her a story. Time didn't permit him to grant her request and Peterson decides to scrap the agenda for the board meeting. Instead, he confesses to working too hard, being inadequate, and to hurrying all the time. Peterson confesses, "I can't do it. I resign."

An astute board member asked him what he wanted to do and he responds with a list that includes being able to read a story to his daughter, Karen, and concludes with these words: "I want to be an unbusy pastor."

But it was the opening line of that list in response to the board member that captured my attention. Peterson stated:

"I want to be a pastor who prays.
I want to be reflective and responsive and
relaxed in the presence of God so that
I can be reflective and responsive and
relaxed in your presence."

When we relax in His presence there is a beautiful opportunity for us to reflect upon His goodness and to offer our praise. Here are a couple of more practical ideas for you as you pray. Consider writing your prayers in a journal. Years ago, I began to teach New Testament classes at the university level. One of my desires for college students in a culture with so much noise was encouraging them to slow down and move from distraction to reflection. Adding a journal to the syllabi for the course created a bit of a mandate, if a student wanted to earn a good grade. I would love to tell you that students flock to this journaling with great joy and all of them love this portion of the course responsibilities. Such is not the case, but what I have seen over the years is a number of students whose lives have been impacted and, in some cases, transformed as they began to write prayers, list prayer requests (and answers), and slowed down and found some moments of stillness.

Henri Nouwen wrote that we need two ministries:

1. A ministry of **presence**
2. A ministry of **absence**

Nouwen said we must "learn to be present with people" and learn the act of "creative withdrawal," also known as being absent. I discovered that I was great at the first – presence and I was terrible at the second - absence. Though better today, I am still more comfortable being present with people than being absent with myself and God.

Here are three things that I believe happen when we are still, really still, still as a stone still:

1. **God's voice gets LOUDER or at least our ears get cleaner.**
2. **God gets BIGGER or at least our vision of Him.**
3. **God's presence becomes CLOSER or at least our awareness of His activity in our lives.**

I promised a couple of ideas so here is the second one, create a prayer reminder. Mine is a piece of leather with a number of inexpensive charms with words, phrases, or symbols purchased at my favorite store, Hobby Lobby. Each object triggers a reminder for me. Here are some examples of my charms:

- Globe – prayers for work of evangelism and discipleship around the world, the persecuted church, and friends serving in some far-off places
- Cross – thanksgiving for God's mercy and grace in my life that is more than amazing
- Love you to the moon and back – my grandchildren who bring so much joy to my life
- Hope – what the world is looking for and a reminder that I can be a hope dispenser
- Faith – now faith, mustard seed faith, mountain-moving faith

Some people carry prayer beads, I carry a collection of charms tied together with leather that allow me to have some structure as I pray for healings and help, hope and hospitality while lifting up praise and Hallelujah to the One who is always waiting for my call.

Let me return to where this chapter started as we bring this little book to a conclusion: **Person that prays or a**

praying person. I'm convinced that the order of the words doesn't matter nearly as much as the practice of prayer. The persistence, the perseverance, the dogged determination that even before we feel like the whole community shows up at our door, we are ready because we have prayed.

In this season of service, I spend many of my days on a university campus. I've discovered that most colleges or universities have a place designated where there are photos of past presidents displayed. Southern Nazarene University, where I serve, is no exception. Our display of past presidents is in a dining room, the President's Dining Room. Fifteen black and white photos hanging on the wall. If I'm honest, most don't look very happy when the photo was taken; some look a little like a mug shot. Since I host a meal or two each week in this dining room, I see the photos often. Beneath each photo is the name of the president, the year their tenure began, a dash, and then the year their time of service as president concluded. A dash doesn't create much of a legacy. And I can only guess what monumental challenges were faced during their tenure. What would it have been like to serve as president during the Great Depression, one of the World Wars, or when interest rates were double digits? The truth is I can't truly know. Some future presidents are going to look at the photos and wonder what it was like to be president during COVID.

Here's what I do know about those presidents on the wall: They prayed, and people prayed for them and for the institution, and we are still around, I believe, because of prayer.

Is there a better legacy for a president or a pastor, a Sunday School teacher, a grandparent, a teacher, a nurse, an attorney, or a street sweeper than to have been a person who called home, often, who prayed for their family, co-workers, strangers, and neighbors?

What might happen if a great host of citizens of another world spent time in this world calling home? The possibilities are powerful. Count me in. I hope you will join me. Call home! Pray big. Pray boldly. Pray often. Pray with passion and compassion. All things are possible when we call home!

REFLECTION QUESTIONS:

1. How would you describe the difference between a person who prays and a praying person? What description best fits you?

2. Where is your favorite time and place to pray? Why?

3. Who or what has had the greatest impact or inspiration on your prayer life?

4. Take a moment and on a piece of paper, write down all of the times in your life when you are absolutely convinced that God communicated a message to you and the only explanation is Him?

5. What's the best piece of wisdom you have ever received about prayer?

6. Do you believe "history belongs to the intercessors?" Why or why not?

7. How might your prayer life move to a deeper and higher level in this next season of life?

ABOUT THE AUTHOR

DR. KEITH NEWMAN was elected as the fifteenth president of Southern Nazarene University in March 2017. With nine years of service as a Houston police officer, seventeen years of pastoral ministry in the Church of the Nazarene, and sixteen years as a senior administrator in Christian higher education, Dr. Newman counts it a great privilege to join a Christ-centered community preparing God-called, purpose-driven, passionate servant leaders who make the world better.

Keith loves to read stories, hear stories, and tell stories, and he believes God is in the middle of all our stories. Spending time with students is at the top of his list of favorite moments each week.

ABOUT SOUTHERN NAZARENE UNIVERSITY

SNU

1899

Founded in 1899, Southern Nazarene University is a private, Christian, liberal arts university—a service of the Church of the Nazarene. Located on a forty-acre campus just west of Oklahoma City, SNU grew out of several small colleges committed to educating people for lives of service to God, leadership, and reconciliation toward their neighbors and within the global community. More than 32,000 alumni work and serve throughout the United States and the world.